D. H. LAWRENCE AND WOMEN

D. H. LAWRENCE AND WOMEN

Carol Dix

ROWMAN AND LITTLEFIELD
Totowa, New Jersey

First published in the United States 1980 by
ROWMAN and LITTLEFIELD
Totowa, N.J.

Library of Congress Cataloging in Publication Data

Dix, Carol M
  D. H. Lawrence and women.

  Bibliography: p.
  Includes index.
  1. Lawrence, David Herbert, 1885-1930--Characters--
Women.   2. Women in literature.   I. Title.
  PR6023.A93Z6238   823'.9'12   79-15235
  ISBN 0-8476-6196-2

Printed in Great Britain

For Allan

Contents

List of Abbreviations

Lawrence works:

WP	*The White Peacock*
SL	*Sons and Lovers*
R	*The Rainbow*
WL	*Women in Love*
LG	*The Lost Girl*
AR	*Aaron's Rod*
K	*Kangaroo*
PS	*The Plumed Serpent*
LCL	*Lady Chatterley's Lover*
JTLJ	*John Thomas and Lady Jane*
ShS	Short Stories
SM	'St Mawr'
VG	'The Virgin and the Gipsy'
SE	Selected Essays
STH	*Study of Thomas Hardy*
P	*Phoenix II*

Other works:

L	*Letters of D. H. Lawrence*
PL	*The Priest of Love*, Harry T. Moore
MG	*The Von Richtofen Sisters*, Martin Green
KM	*Sexual Politics*, Kate Millett
EC	*D. H. Lawrence and Edward Carpenter*, Emile Delavenay
Dal	*The Forked Flame*, H. M. Daleski
SS	*D. H. Lawrence: The World of the Major Novels*, Scott Saunders
NM	*The Prisoner of Sex*, Norman Mailer

Introduction

Ursula, perhaps the major character in all Lawrence's fiction, as she appears in *The Rainbow*, has been my *alter ego*, mentor and guide, since teenage years. I first read *The Rainbow* as a schoolgirl, in a small Midlands industrial town, just like the one in which Ursula lived. Naturally, I related very strongly to the young woman's emotional and spiritual needs. Ursula, I have since reasoned, plays such an important part in Lawrence's writing because she was used to represent the author himself – to reflect his emotional and spiritual needs. But for me it was the Ursula who dreamed of getting out of that Midlands town – who felt claustrophobic about the social limitations on her life; who fought her parents to get a job; who played with men and sex, wanting to experiment in life; who believed in love and passion, and hoped desperately to find it; who ended up in the novel standing on the threshold, looking beyond, believing there was a different way of life – who summed up the growing feelings within myself.

Little did I know, at that time, that there was indeed a world out there, a different way of life. As I was growing up, the social limitations began to be forced off and the horizons, particularly for young women, were immeasurably widened. As I have recorded in another book, the social mores that so trapped Ursula were lifted one by one. The Women's Movement of the early seventies exploded, with more force perhaps than the suffragette movement of Ursula's time – and with it came the prospect of freedom to young women.

Those freedoms in my own life meant that, unlike Ursula, I was able to leave my small town and home background, go to university with no parental opposition, and enter into a profession of my own choosing, as long as I could then make the grade. I read literature at university, and took my undergraduate degree, smiling; but then I ran as fast as I could from the doors of academe. The wide, free world beckoned me, as it had done Ursula. Not for me the life of an academic. I became a journalist. I began to write books. I still do not want to stop exploring the limits of those widened horizons.

Why I should have wanted to return to literary studies, to write this book on Lawrence, has been asked many times. It all came about because of Ursula. Kate Millett's *Sexual Politics* was part of our required reading in the early seventies. Much as I sympathised with any feminist notion in those days, I could not dispel my unhappiness with her misjudgement of Lawrence. It was from the pages of Lawrence that I had learned so much relevant to my life. I felt the need to look at his writing in greater depth again.

From there, the idea miraculously took root. A brief reread of the novels only confirmed my suspicions. There was so much to be said on the subject of Lawrence and women, that had been missed out in previous critical works, or, at least, had never been brought together between the same hard covers. I jotted the idea down and found Macmillans, by accident, noticing that they were producing a list of relevant books – critical literary works, written by women, re-assessing traditional critical viewpoints through their contemporary enlightened eyes. The idea was sent to my editor at Macmillans. He liked it. The book was signed up and only then did I realise what an enormous task I had taken on.

Two and a half years later, I still feel hesitant about the under-taking. I am by now a long way removed from the academic world, and do not feel I can write in their style. On the other hand, I hold out no over-zealous respect for their academic writing or jargon. My approach is therefore that of the lay person, with a degree and a career as a writer behind her, not that of a literary critic. I hope the book will be readable and enjoyable to those of pure academic bent, and to those with a broader outlook as well. Having been in journal-ism for the last nine years, I cannot get away from the notion that writing is meant to entertain and distract, not merely inform.

The one theme running through my book is that, far from degrading women, far from treating them as inferior objects, as Lawrence is accused of by Kate Millett, he saw more in women, and the feminine principle, than did most of his contemporaries. A far-seeing man, Lawrence created female characters who were finally to emerge as real people in the sixties and seventies – some fifty years after his death. For that I wish to thank him. In a letter, discussing the proposed project he then called *The Sisters*, which became the two novels, *The Rainbow* and *Women in Love*, Lawrence said that he was working on the idea of woman 'becoming individual, self-responsible, taking her own initiative'. It is that very concept and its implications so relevant to men and women today, that provided for me the interest and desire to write the book.

London, May 1978 CAROL DIX

Acknowledgements

The author and publisher wish to thank the following who have kindly given permission for the use of copyright material: Lawrence Pollinger Ltd and Farrar, Straus & Giroux, Inc. for the extracts from *The Priest of Love* by Harry T. Moore; Lawrence Pollinger Ltd and Alfred A. Knopf, Inc. for the extracts from *The Plumed Serpent*; Lawrence Pollinger Ltd on behalf of the Estate of the late Mrs Frieda Lawrence Ravagli, and Viking Penguin Inc. for the extracts from the works of D. H. Lawrence; and Weidenfeld (Publishers) Ltd for the extracts from *The Prisoner of Sex* by Norman Mailer.

1 Background: Social Upheaval and Women

Lawrence as a writer was a man gifted with original ideas. The world he grew up in is of utmost importance in any study of his thinking. Lawrence was influenced by and subject to the major intellectual forces of his day. He was also part of the cultural history of his time. The fact that he was able to break those bounds in his thinking is all the more to his credit. It is to the historical background, and evidence from Lawrence's own writings and letters, that we must first look for the roots of his ideas.

Lawrence arrived independently at the major widely held views of both philosophy and psychology; the world he entered as a young man was a world on fire with intellectual breakthroughs: whether caused by Freud, Herbert Spencer, Darwin's *Origin of the Species*, Huxley's *Man's Place in Nature*, Ernest Haekel's *The Riddle of the Universe*, John Stuart Mill, or even just Shaw and Wells. Lawrence read anthropology – Taylor and Frazer, Jane Harrison and Gilbert Murray were known to him – which is not surprising as any young person alive to new ideas catches up on the contemporary reading of his times.

The most significant transition in ideas happening at that time, at the turn of the century up to the First World War, was that connected with the role and place of women. J. S. Mill's *Subjection of Women* had come out in 1869; the Married Women's Property Act was legalised in 1882. Both Shaw and Ibsen had already popularised the theories in their plays. Ibsen's *The Doll's House* had opened in London in 1889, shattering the world with Nora's great door slam for the independence of women. *Rosmersholm* and *Hedda Gabler* were both in London in 1891; and Shaw's *Mrs Warren's Profession* hit the London stage in 1893, with its admission that women's sole occupation should no longer be limited to marriage. Whatever he felt about modern woman, Shaw had seen that it was necessary for women to have the right to work and to enter the professions. Shaw

(Brown, 1975, Chapter 6) himself was an attractive advanced figure of the 1890s. He befriended a woman like Eleanor Marx, who lived with Edward Aveling rather than marry him (though she committed suicide later when he dropped her for another woman). Shaw also corresponded with the actress Janet Achurch, with Ellen Terry and with Mrs Patrick Campbell, the lady who had held the 1890s society with her fiery temper, rare wit and biting tongue. But Shaw, by his thirties, would say that the women he met were 'unwomanly', trying for careers in the arts but with little chance of getting on. He had a long intellectual friendship with Annie Besant, who offered to live with him; in sin, because her husband was still alive. She presented Shaw with her own contract for a free love partnership. Shaw backed out because he could see no freedom in it for himself.

During the final decades of the nineteenth century, and the first decade of the twentieth century, things changed. Women's education (SS, pp. 42–7) had expanded faster than anything else in the society around them, so women knew what was available to them but were frustrated in their attempts to take advantage – either in the professions or in a way of life that would be financially independent of marriage. They were politically impotent, and in many ways still emotionally impotent. These were the strong contradictions that led to the violent and militant first push of the feminist movement. The period 1903–14 was the prime time of Mrs Pankhurst's Women's Social and Political Union. Demonstrations by suffragettes were very common in the London of those years and so, while Lawrence lived in Croydon as a teacher, he could not help but be exposed to this intellectual furore. It was in Croydon he drafted *Sons and Lovers*, and in his letters of that time he treated suffragettes as a normal part of the political landscape. After all, his own mother, and his earliest female friend, Jessie Chambers, had both expressed the very same frustrations now being expressed on a wider scale. And later female friends, Louie Burrows and Alice Dax, were quite adamant in their views. In a letter to Louie Burrows, 28 March 1909, he described a Croydon by-election involving an anti-suffrage Conservative. He wrote that he had seen a crowd of men round two suffragettes in a car. One, a Miss Cameron, shouted 'If the men cannot control themselves, it is time women had some power to control them'. The howling mob tried to overturn the car, and the violent episode obviously had its effect on Lawrence.

It is obvious from the novels that he understood how young women of his acquaintance were affected by suffragettism. In *Sons and Lovers*, Clara – partly fashioned on Louie Burrows and partly on Alice Dax – meets Paul for a theatre visit. He describes her: 'She was with one of her suffragette friends. She wore an old long coat, which did not suit her, and had a little wrap over her head, which she hated.' Lawrence critics (KM, pp. 237–93) who maintain he hated suffragettes use this description to prove their point. But I read it more straightforwardly. Lawrence had seen how young women espoused the cause and, because of it, that they began to adopt a style of dress that was no longer flattering. He was not criticising Louie Burrows, or Clara Dawes, for doing so. After all, it was Clara who taught young Paul Morel the ways of the world and he had a lot to admire in her.

The movements for social change in the Britain of 1910–14 (SS, pp. 42–7) were dominated by the Fabianism of Shaw and the Webbs, by Mrs Pankhurst's feminism, the liberal reformism associated with Lloyd-George, the scientific utopianism of H. G. Wells, the Labour movement of Arthur Henderson, Soreliam syndicalism, and revolutionary socialism. The young Lawrence was not exactly at the hub of this intellectual giantism, but he was there on the fringes, soaking it all in. We know how interested he was in current ideas, because of the information that has come from the past about the intellectual meetings held in his home town, Eastwood, near Nottingham, which Lawrence attended. They were run by his friends William and Sallie Hopkin, and the story has been told very eloquently by their daughter Enid Hopkin Hilton in a letter to Harry T. Moore (PL, pp. 154–5). It was through these Eastwood meetings that Lawrence first became exposed to ideas discussed in the heat of that sitting room; and to women who espoused the ideas with much more vehemence than their men. Sallie Hopkin was an undoubted influence, but more so was the rather mysterious, and none the less intriguing, figure of Alice Dax, who played such an important part in young Lawrence's emotional and intellectual development.

Enid Hilton describes the Eastwood meetings: 'Every Sunday evening was open house, when my mother served wonderful "snacks", and we had music, talk, readings, or just plain fun. Philip Snowden, Ramsay MacDonald, Charlotte Despard, Annie Kenny, Beatrice and Sydney Webb, and others of the then "forward" group visited us frequently and these Lawrence met. He was a silent listener or an almost violent leader of the conversation.' About Alice Dax she had yet more to say. She was married to Henry Dax, a pharmacist who settled in Eastwood, and later became an occultist.

In 1912 they moved to Mansfield. Henry Dax was a conservative sort of man, in personality and business, and he stuck to the routine medicines, until Alice introduced him to the more frivolous sales of combs and brushes. Alice is often mentioned as the model for Clara Dawes, in *Sons and Lovers*; but there is also a lot of Kate Leslie, in *The Plumed Serpent*, in her independent, mature, very self-contained form of womanhood. Enid Hilton writes,

> Alice Dax and my mother were *years* ahead of their time (which may have been one of her attractions for DHL), and both were widely read, 'advanced' in dress, thought and house decoration. Alice was almost completely uninhibited in an age when you just weren't . . . Part of her fight against the 'clutter' of her generation showed itself in her refusal to have one unnecessary article or item in her home. There were few pictures, only one rug, no knick-knacks collected over the years, no items of beauty or arresting interest, but lots of *tidy* books . . . The floors were linoleum-covered or of polished wood. It reflected Alice – clear, direct, uncluttered in thought and action, to the point of harshness . . . Together, she and my mother worked for the women's cause, and I remember being taken to 'meetings' in the City of Nottingham. We waved green, purple and white flags and the speakers, the Pankhursts, Annie Kenny and others whose names I have forgotten – came home with us and stayed at our house, and discussions went on far into the night, intense, but friendly and a bit gay . . . Keir Hardy stayed with us, Ramsay MacDonald, Philip Snowden, Ernest Carpenter, Margaret Bondfield – many others. Mother was an amazing hostess and our house was 'open' every Sunday evening . . . Alice Dax carried her ideas almost to extremes. Gradually she became a NAME in the district, a person to whom people turned in trouble, and who initiated all the good community enterprises, such as nursing associations, local forms of health insurance and so forth . . . She successfully tackled the school system too, and new modern schools arose. Alice Dax was one of the kindest persons I have ever met, but most of the men of her generation feared her. She represented a kind of ramrod, forcing the future into their present in an uncomfortable and uncomprehended manner. And she could and did contradict their statements and words of wisdom, and she *dared* to be right – too often. So my father, I feel, subconsciously feared the impact of her personality and beliefs on my mother, and on me. As with

most reformers he could change the world but liked his home intact (PL, pp. 155–6).

Alice Dax becomes important because of her relationship with Lawrence. She fell in love with him and, in fact, it was Alice who first introduced the young Lawrence to sex – a desire that had proved such a problem to him since the nice young girls, like Jessie Chambers, still felt the need for marriage first. It took a liberated woman, a suffragette interested in the ideas of free love, to be free enough to help Lawrence. Willie Hopkin tells this story (PL, p. 149), of how he overheard Alice Dax tell Mrs Hopkin, 'Sallie, I gave Bert sex. I had to. He was over at our house, struggling with a poem he couldn't finish, so I took him upstairs and gave him sex. He came downstairs and finished the poem.' Alice loved Lawrence to an extent she had never loved a man before. She hoped the child she conceived then was his, though it was her husband's. The story goes that, after Lawrence, she never had sex again, with her husband or anyone. She let Lawrence go for his own good, knowing that as she was often in opposition with him she feared their quarrelsome relationship would be bad for him. Alice wrote to Frieda Lawrence in 1935, after Lawrence's death, that she knew he had found the right mate. 'I was never meant for him and what he liked was not the me I *was*, but the me I might have been – the potential me which would never have struggled to life but for his help and influence.' Enid Hilton has said that Alice went through a hell of 'the sort we can barely imagine'. We can somehow imagine it, after reading Lawrence's novels, in which he describes the trap felt by young women of those days, stuck in small grey mining towns, with insensitive husbands who fed them neither sexual, nor spiritual, life – think of Connie Chatterley before she met Parkin/Mellors.

Alice was no doubt a major intellectual influence on Lawrence, and it might have been she who introduced him to the writings of Edward Carpenter (EC, pp. 11–23) who, if not a direct influence on Lawrence, certainly came at an auspiciously contemporary time in cultural history. Carpenter first put the ideas of homosexuality, and the liberation of sexuality, into print and earned much scorn and contempt for his courage in so doing. His essays, collected as *Love's Coming of Age*, include chapters on 'The sex passion'; 'Man – the ungrown'; 'Woman, the serf'; 'Woman in freedom'; 'Marriage, a retrospect'; and 'Marriage, a forecast – the free society' which put together read like the theory behind Lawrence's fiction. On women, Edward Carpenter said 'What woman most needs today . . . is a basis for independence for her life' which will enable her to 'face man on an equality . . . and to dispose of herself and her sex perfectly freely'. His ideas were too frank for polite society to acknowledge openly, but the book went into twenty editions and was secretly, at least, very popular. He was the first to say that sex was something to be enjoyed – by men and women. Carpenter's influence will be explored later in this book. For now, it is interesting to speculate, as Delavenay does in *D. H. Lawrence and Edward Carpenter*, how Lawrence might have read him without ever publicly saying he had.

Alice Dax had all Carpenter's books. It is known that she lent Jessie Chambers *Love's Coming of Age*, in the winter 1909–10. The friendship of Alice and Jessie is mirrored in the friendship of Miriam and Clara in *Sons and Lovers*. For example, it is Clara who tells Paul to try with Miriam 'the great experiment of sex'. Alice was a voracious reader of books and an emancipated woman who freely 'gave Bert sex'. Even Alice's doctrine of lack of decoration of her house, 'simplification of life', was a Carpenter doctrine. It does seem likely that she would have lent Lawrence the same books as she lent young Jessie. Edward Carpenter, we know, eventually read Lawrence. He said of *The Rainbow* (EC, pp. 11–23), not very flatteringly, 'The style is jerky and rather "forced" . . . as you say his drawing of women is good'.

Delavenay feels that by showing the link between Lawrence's ideas, and psychology, and Carpenter's, he will also be showing that Lawrence was essentially pre-Freudian, closer to the evolution of the declining years of the nineteenth century, than to the discoveries or theories which spread widely in the second quarter of the twentieth century. Not, he says, non-Freudian, but not dependent on Freud. The whole question of whether Lawrence was directly influenced by Freud has become hot debate. For the facts of his direct knowledge, we can turn to Frieda Lawrence, who said in 1942, a long time after his death:

> Lawrence knew about Freud before he wrote the final draft of *Sons and Lovers*. I don't know whether he had read Freud or heard of him before we met, in 1912. But I was a great Freud admirer; we had long arguments and Lawrence's conclusion was more or less that Freud looked on sex too much from the doctor's point of

view, that Freud's 'sex' and 'libido' were too limited and
mechanical and that the root was deeper.

Lawrence did meet and befriend official Freudians in 1914; Dr David
Eder and Barbara Law. But then Frieda is also under-emphasising
the effects of Freudian psychology on the day. Its effect was
extremely powerful and subtle.

Psychology and the new science of sociology (SS, pp. 74) were
among the most powerful influences at that time: they were behind
the artistic experiments that were to develop with Picasso, the music
of Schoenberg. It was the time of Weber in sociology, Einstein in
physics, and Russell and Wittgenstein in philosophy. When
Lawrence was a young man and writer, depth psychology, with its
emphasis on impersonal forces at play on the individual, was not
outspoken, but the beginnings were in the air. What Lawrence
himself has to say on the subject comes from his later writings,
particularly the long essays 'Fantasia of the Unconscious' and
'Psychoanalysis and the Unconscious' (1929). For a direct statement,
we need look no further than his 'Foreword to *Women in Love*' (P, pp.
275–7), in which he says of that novel, 'In point of style, fault is often
found with the continual slightly modified repetition. The only
answer is that it is natural to the author and that every natural crisis
in emotion or passion or understanding comes from this pulsing,
frictional, to-and-fro, which works up to culmination.'

But to return to Frieda, she was surely the one major influence on
Lawrence's life, in every way. Frieda was not just the woman who
inspired Lawrence's fancy and feelings about love, so that they ran
away together and stuck by each other more or less until his death.
She was also the person who gave reason to his quiescent theories
on love and sex, coming as she did from the more advanced literary
and intellectual milieu of Germany. When Lawrence met Frieda it
was she who was sleepwalking, having been married to Professor
Ernest Weekly, French teacher at Nottingham, for twelve years,
borne him three children, and suffered the grim and restricting life
of the provincial housewife. Frieda was 32 and dead, compared to
her former youthful self.

Frieda von Richtofen had grown up with her two sisters, Else and
Nusch, in Germany. As teenage girls they had enjoyed first of all the
attentions of the young men of the Kaiser's court, and then of the
young idealists of intellectual Munich (MG, 1974). Frieda described
herself as 'a wild child, and they could not tame me, those gentle

nuns' (at her convent school). Later John Middleton Murry said of
Frieda, she 'was a completely emancipated woman. Equality of the
sexes she took in her stride, which reached daily a little further still
. . . her experience of male authority (from her Prussian father) was
seen . . . in disintegration'. Frieda's motives in marrying Weekly are
hard to work out, unless the idea of going to live in England with a
noted intellectual was attraction enough. Her sister Else, mean-
while, was living the life of the new woman, to an extent that
English women dared not. Else had been one of the first female
students at Heidelberg and wrote a doctorate on the relations of
political parties to social insurance laws, under the direction of Max
Weber. She married one of her teachers at Heidelberg, Edgar Jaffe, a
professor of political economy, and later became Weber's mistress.
Weber himself had, as his wife, the notable Marianne Weber, who
wrote in an essay in 1909, 'Authority and Autonomy in Marriage',
that women feel the need to work with men, to build together with
them in a world of culture. Eight years later, however, poor
Marianne had seen what else happens as women grow older. She
called the essay 'The Personality Change in Women Students', and
described the change from militancy to ultra-femininity when love
became paramount. She was referring to the new movement towards eroticism, in those years, which she saw as a threat to
women.

   During these same years, Frieda's marriage had deteriorated and
her feelings were being stultified in it. Her first affair was with a
Nottingham lace manufacturer, who used to take her to Sherwood
Forest in one of the earliest cars. Her one serious affair began on a
visit to the family in Germany in 1907, when she met Otto Gross, a
disciple of Freud's. She fell in love, and began a long-distance
relationship which lasted several years. Gross was a noted thinker
of the Munich group of intellectuals, known as the Schwabing
Circle, who had very pronounced ideas on women, on love, and on
man/woman relations; above all, on sex and eroticism. To love
erotically, he contended, was not to feel identified with the other
person, but with the third being, the relationship itself. Erotic love
alone can finally overcome man's loneliness. Relationship understood as that third thing, worshipped as a supreme value, will allow
the lover to combine an erotic union with an uncompromised drive
to individuality. Those ideas are very close to Lawrence's.

   The Schwabing Circle (MG, p. 73), or *die komische Runde*, was a
centre of ideas and thinkers – Alfred Schuler, Ludwig Klages, Karl

Wolfskeh and Stefan George – during the years 1893–1903. They met to discuss anthropology and cultural history, patriarchal values of the west, life values, eroticism, the value of myth and primitive cultures, instinct and intuition over science. They also argued for the primacy of the female mode of being – working from the influence of Bachofen's writings on matriarchy. The state, said an ideas man like Gross, represses sexuality, or forces sexual energy to be misused so that you can have a whole nation of hysterical women and aggressive men. The state was inherently homosexual in its authoritarianism.

This was the Frieda whom Lawrence met; the woman who had been involved with Gross for over eight years, who must, complicitly, have adhered to Gross's ideas. She, like Lawrence, would have been looking for love, and for a relationship with a man through which she could put those ideas into practice. As Martin Green says, 'The *komische Runde* described the woman it wanted, and Frieda Weekly answered the appeal . . . and Lawrence was its heir'. It was Lawrence who took those ideas on and made something real out of them – from which we have all been influenced.

2 The Feminine Point of View

'I think the one thing to do, is for man to have courage to draw nearer to women . . . be altered by them, (L, 2 June 1914).

Lawrence wrote this in one of his letters for the year 1914; letters written home from his travels and exile with Frieda, in which he so often tried to explain the thinking and development of his ideas. One very central thought through the correspondence is that of the 'female mode of being' or of the feminisation of the world into which Lawrence saw the west entering. It was an idea that he had previously conceived in his own head, and to which, through Frieda, he was able to give new birth. A lot of Lawrence's subject matter relates very strongly to the importance of the 'feminine' and – putting into its rightful place – the 'masculine' in the world of art, ideas and action. It is a trend that has indeed continued in the twentieth century and can be seen in more recent attempts towards redefining life, morals and values in anti-war movements, and the growing sympathy with women's emancipation.

The Cosmic Circle of Schwabing, which Lawrence came to know through Frieda, had as one of its precepts the importance of the 'female mode of being'. In their turn, they had been influenced by the Swiss scholar Bachofen and his ideas on matriarchy. Lawrence probably never read *Das Mutterecht*, as written by Bachofen. Frieda, however, embodied the matriarchal ideal, learned from Otto Gross, so Lawrence was living out Bachofen's ideas, enacting in practical life the female mode of being. Lawrence also came across the notable Max Weber, through Frieda's sister Else, and in him saw painfully enacted the male mode of being. Lawrence was already antipathetic to 'male' action; whereas Weber was trying to redefine 'manhood'. As Martin Green has said (MG, p. 117), 'Lawrence was making himself into a "man-and-woman", exploring with great boldness the female mode of being . . .'. Where Lawrence tended to agree with Max Weber, and others of the patriarchy, over the newly emerging women's movement, was that Lawrence saw this as inducing women into the male mode of being; seducing women to becoming part of the male world of action, work, ideas, war, coldness and lack of emotion or instinct. Lawrence wanted women to go somewhere beyond that.

A clue to the influence of Bachofen's matriarchal ideas on Lawrence can be found in comparing some of their theories. In *Das Mutterecht*, Bachofen says about Urr religion:

> The Mother is earlier than the son. The feminine has priority, while masculine creativity only appears afterwards as a secondary phenomenon . . . he exists only in perishable form. Woman exists from everlasting, self-subsistent, immutable . . . Ever the same Great Mother mates with ever new men.

Lawrence himself wrote about Genesis:

> The whole chronology is upside down: the Word created Man, and Man lay down and gave birth to Woman, whereas we know the Woman lay in travail, and gave birth to Man, who in his hour uttered his word . . . The woman is the Flesh. She produces all the rest of the flesh, including the intermediary pieces called man (MG, p.83).

For Lawrence's further theories on the theme of 'feminisation', we can turn to his *Study of Thomas Hardy* (STH, 1973) in which we find all the ideas, sometimes incoherently, put together. Lawrence was beginning to express ideas which women themselves have picked up much more strongly in recent years. He saw the time of change around the corner. He felt that it was time for man to become more passive and woman more active. Within this theory, he saw the answer to art and to his own creative spirit: 'This is the desire of every man . . . that the woman of his body shall be the begetter of his whole life, that she, in her female spirit, shall beget in him his ideas, his motion, himself' (STH, p.   ). Man can only find his art by finding the woman in himself. When Lawrence and Frieda ran away together, to travel in Europe, they were running away from this particular form of western civilisation; disillusioned by war, by factories, by mining and with what men had done for the world. On 2 June 1914, he wrote his famous letter containing his theory of artistic creation:

I think the only re-sourcing of art, revivifying it, is to make it more the joint work of man and woman. I think the one thing to do, is for men to have courage to draw nearer to women, expose themselves to them, and be altered by them; and for women to admit and accept men . . . (L, 2 June 1914).

There are in fact strong indications that Lawrence, in his novels, wrote from the feminine point of view. One of the themes of this book is that Lawrence treats women with a respect hardly ever accorded them by male writers, let alone female writers. To Lawrence, it is women who explore, progress, advance, think and feel. The real heroes of all his novels are the women. Male characters never have such big parts to play, nor are they seen so wholly and roundly. The men turn up and perform as secondary characters, relating to the women, or needed by them as props. Women characters figure often in his titles and predominate in the subject matter. Also, it is easy to see that when Lawrence is writing about himself, with the exception of Paul Morel in *Sons and Lovers*, he puts himself in the guise of one of the female characters. Ursula, of the *The Rainbow*, is the most obvious. Young women of Lawrence's day were experiencing, more than his contemporary males, the need to break out into a new way of life, to exile themselves, to break the ties of belonging. Lawrence understood women, and the novels are written from that feminine point of view.

Whether one can say adamantly that Lawrence is writing about himself in his novels, through the female character, has to some degree been answered by the novelist himself in his other writings. In one such work, the 'Foreword to *Women in Love*', published well after his death in 1936, in the American edition, written in an attempt to answer the charges of eroticism aimed at him about the novel, Lawrence explains much about the writer's role in tracing his own attitudes and ideas.

This novel pretends only to be a record of the writer's own desires, aspirations, struggles; in a word, a record of the profoundest experiences in the self. Nothing that comes from the deep, passional soul is bad, or can be bad . . .

Any man of real individuality tries to know and to understand what is happening, even in himself, as he goes along. This struggle for verbal consciousness should not be left out in art. It is a very great part of life. It is not superimposition of a theory. It is the passionate struggle into conscious being (P, pp. 275–7).

Lawrence widened his defence by saying, 'We are now in a period of crisis. Every man who is acutely alive is acutely wrestling with his own soul. The people that can bring forth the new passion, the new idea, this people will endure.'

It is very important to see this side of Lawrence before approaching the novels. It throws a completely different light on the female characters and increases their significance. Lawrence was intrinsically writing about the liberation of the self, so he could relate that to young women of his day and to himself. Not only is Ursula reaching out but, in *Women in Love*, her sister Gudrun also assumes an independent role: that of the artist. Gudrun becomes Birkin's *alter ego*; or Lawrence's. They have both moved about a great deal, life seeming uncertain, with no definite rhythms. She 'was one of life's outcasts, one of the drifting lives that have no root'. Like Lawrence, Gudrun is an artist, alienated from her Midlands background, attracted and repelled at the same time by London's bohemia, and also, like Birkin, attracted by dark, sensual men. *Women in Love* is the very beginning of Lawrence's other need to express, through the feminine point of view, his own adoration of men. Through Gudrun he expresses his feelings about Gerald; which brings us to the tricky problem of Lawrence's homosexual theme through the novels, which we will return to later. Daleski, in *The Forked Flame*, said,

> It is my contention that Lawrence, though believing intensely in himself as a male, was fundamentally identified with the female principle as he himself defines it in the essay on Hardy . . . I believe that Lawrence initially made a strenuous effort to reconcile the male and female elements in himself but that he was more strongly feminine than masculine and that he was unable to effect such reconciliation (Dal, 1965, p. 13).

Or, as Daleski puts it more forcefully, 'Lawrence was a woman in a man's skin'.

Before we join the bandwagon proclaiming Lawrence a homosexual, thus proving he hated women, I believe we should stop and consider just what period of time Lawrence was living in. The ideas he was battling with link with today's more common views on the essential androgyny of all human beings; that coming to terms with oneself is coming to terms with the masculine and feminine in each of us. Liberation of the individual will eventually mean getting away from sex role stereotypes and enable us to perceive what mixtures we all are. Lawrence made this his standpoint; but sometimes it was difficult to make a stand for it in a society that desperately disapproved of such ideas. Women were only just coming out. It was not widely accepted that they had anything much to offer. For instance, one of his early reviewers in *The Athenaeum* said of *The White Peacock*, somewhat disparagingly, 'This novel is characteristic of the modern fiction which is being written by the feminine hand because it uses "cinematographic" methods – cleverness in his "modern study of nerves" '.

Then, there is the question of whether Lawrence knew of the writings of Edward Carpenter, of *Love's Coming of Age* – which was the coming-out of the homosexual theme in literature at the same time as being an urgent call to liberate both sexes so that they could find their sexuality and their individuality. If Lawrence remained ignorant of Carpenter, despite his friendship with Alice Dax, then it is remarkable that the two men were living more or less contemporaneously. Carpenter described the future male as being of 'intermediate sex'. Birkin, in *Women in Love*, is a deliberately ambivalent male, much closer to some notion of a future ideal male than to the commonly held view of masculinity. Carpenter maintained that the common male, 'half-grown' was a 'tyrant' and that he had made woman a 'serf, prostitute, lady or drudge'. Carpenter wrote well on the changing role of women, and the effect of feminisation on the world as a whole:

> In the West, the modern upgrowth of Woman and her influence will ere long make possible a Humanity which shall harmonise even in each individual the masculine and feminine elements, and bring back at last the Brain and the self-conscious mind into relation with that immense storehouse of age-long knowledge and power which is represented by the physical body of the individual, as it is represented by the communal life and instinct in the mass-people (EC, p. 134).

Carpenter's search was quite directly for the mix of male and female, the balance, in the individual. So was Lawrence's, if less explicitly so.

Of the women in Lawrence's novels, Emily, George's sister in *The White Peacock*, is the first to express Lawrence's point of view. Emily was probably fashioned to some degree after Louie Burrows, but in her expression of joy in independence it is Lawrence himself who comes across. Emily, like Lawrence, gets away from small-town life, to London, where she teaches. She lives in digs, as did Lawrence in his Croydon years, and writes back to her friend Cyril: 'At home you cannot live your own life. You have to struggle to keep even a little part for yourself . . . It is such a relief not to be anything to anybody, but just to please yourself . . . I have begun to write a story' (WP, p. 299).

In *Sons and Lovers*, obviously, it is Paul who is Lawrence himself. But Paul is an interesting young male character in his own right, a precursor of Birkin who is trying to sort out his feelings and attitudes. Paul is described as finding men 'common and rather dull', 'The girls all liked to hear him talk . . . They all liked him, and he adored them' (SL, p. 138). Paul, like Lawrence, was finding more to interest him, intellectually and spiritually, in young women than in young men. He was more akin to them, himself more like a woman than a man. In *The Rainbow*, there are many such clues and pointers; beginning with the epic quote about the Brangwen woman who 'faced outwards . . . to enlarge their own scope and range and freedom' (R, p. 9). The whole novel is a quest for the coming-out of feminine consciousness.

Anna Brangwen is also a good example of the young Lawrence, in her feelings of claustrophobia. She thinks of the torture cell, as a teenage girl, in which the victim could not stand or stretch out, 'she could feel the horror of the crampedness, as something very real' (R, p. 106). Then it is young Tom's turn to mirror Lawrence. He is described very carefully, as a Lawrentian man, 'He had a quick intelligence. From the High School he went to London to study . . . He had a subtle, quick, critical intelligence, a mind that was like a scale or balance. There was something of a woman in all this' (R, p. 240) – a significant comment for Lawrence to make about this early male character. He expands the idea by adding. 'He and his mother had a kind of affinity' (R, p. 241). And, later, Tom had given way to 'the little matriarchy . . . nursing the child and helping with the housework, indifferent any more of his own dignity and importance . . . He was not what is called a manly man: he did not drink or smoke or arrogate importance' (R, p. 208). Lawrence is not criticising him here. These were the changing roles he was experiencing.

Ursula is perhaps the one most important character to reflect this theme, as the very embodiment of Lawrence on the journey through life. At grammar school in Nottingham, she yearns to escape from narrow provincial life, 'the belittling circumstances of life, the little jealousies, the little differences, the little meannesses . . .'. 'So even as a girl of twelve she was glad to burst the narrow boundary of Cossethay, where only limited people lived' (R, pp. 263–4). Ursula's independence which cuts her off from her background and environment is often dealt with: 'There was the mysterious man's world to be adventured upon, the world of daily work and duty, and existence as a working member of the community' (R, pp. 334).

Ursula, too, experienced the joy and wonder of learning, of art, of expanding her horizons, which we know Lawrence felt;

> She wanted so many things. She wanted to read great, beautiful books, and be rich with them; she wanted to see beautiful things, and have the joy of them for ever; she wanted to know big, free people; and there remained always the want she could put no name to (R, p. 406).

It is in Ursula that we see the necessity of cutting oneself off from parents, even country, if the individual is ever to break free and form her, or him, self. This was very much Lawrence's own plight:

> she repeated: 'I have no father nor mother nor lover, I have no allocated place in the world of things, I do not belong to Beldover nor to Nottingham nor to England nor to this world, they none of them exist, I am trammelled and entangled in them, but they are all unreal' (R, p. 493).

And, in *Women in Love*, when Ursula and Birkin leave England to go travelling together, it is very similar to Lawrence and Frieda's own escape:

> What had she to do with parents and antecedents? She knew herself new and unbegotten, she had no father, no mother, no anterior connections, she was herself, pure and silvery, she belonged only to the oneness with Birkin, a oneness that struck deeper notes, sounding into the heart of the universe, the heart of reality, where she had never existed before (WL, p. 460).

Gudrun, in *Women in Love*, as has already been discussed, takes over for the Lawrentian figure from Ursula, as artist, exile, and loner in society. Through Gudrun, Lawrence expresses his views on the importance of finding a 'female art'. He sees it as the pure, sensuous art, of feeling and experience. Gudrun is allowed to see her lovers merely as the fuel for this subtle knowledge. Through love, she will experience such deep feelings; 'a female art, the art of pure, perfect knowledge in sensuous understanding' (WL, p. 505). Alvina in *The Lost Girl*, is also Lawrence, in her escape from the claustrophobia of Midlands life, running away to Italy, experiencing the ripeness of life there – the dangers of throwing oneself into life and love, and the richness to be achieved if you risk the danger.

Through Birkin, in *Women in Love*, Lawrence tries to describe the modern male, the future version of manhood he sees for a new world, in which men and women have come nearer to each other. Then, in the ensuing novels, *Aaron's Rod, The Plumed Serpent* and *Kangaroo*, Lawrence digresses, in his middle age, to a different theme of manliness, that will be dealt with in later chapters. In *John Thomas and Lady Jane*, however (the second version of *Lady Chatterley*), Lawrence returns to his former stronger theories. He gives Connie these words to Parkin, expressing Lawrence's views on 'manliness' and this new version of manhood:

> 'Why do you mind?' she said, tears coming to her eyes. 'It's foolish! You say you have too much of a woman in you, you only mean you are more sensitive than stupid people like Dan Coutts. You ought to be proud that you are sensitive, and have that much of a woman's good qualities. It's very good for a man to have a touch of woman's sensitiveness. I hate your stupid, hard-headed clowns who think they are so very *manly*' (JTLJ, p. 333).

So, if we face a critic of Lawrence's attitude towards women, such as Kate Millett, fairly with the evidence of his very real interest in feminisation, the new female mode of being, the new awareness of androgyny, the arguments disappear before our eyes. For a very good discussion of the possible psychology motivating the ideas of Lawrence, I turn to Norman Mailer's refutation of Millett's theories in *The Prisoner of Sex*, in which he discusses the writer in these terms, 'never had a male novelist written so intimately about women'. I find Mailer's character assessment of Lawrence very perceptive; in its own way it puts paid to earlier theories that had been written and deduced in ignorance of Lawrence's true interest. The ideas that so engaged Lawrence have become common parlance by Norman Mailer's days:

> Yet he was a man more beautiful perhaps than we can guess, and it is worth the attempt to try to perceive the logic of his life, for he illumines the passion to be masculine as no other writer, he reminds us of the beauty of desiring to be a man, for he was not much of a man himself, a son despised by his father, beloved of his mother, boy and young man and prematurely aging writer with the soul of a beautiful woman. It is not only that no other man writes so well about women, but indeed is there a woman who can?

> . . . So, yes, Lawrence understood women as they had never been understood before, understood them with all the tortured fever of a man who had the soul of a beautiful, imperious and passionate woman, yet he was locked into the body of a middling male physique, not physically strong, of reasonable good looks, pleasant to somewhat seedy-looking man, no stud. What a nightmare to balance that soul! to take the man in himself, locked from youth into every need for profound female companionship, a man almost wholly oriented toward the company of women, and attempt to go out into the world of men, indeed even dominate the world of men, so that he might find a balance.

> . . . His mother had adored him. Since his first sense of himself as a male had been in the tender air of her total concern – now, and always, his strength would depend upon just such outsize admiration. Dominance over women was not tyranny to him but equality, for dominance was the indispensable elevator which would raise his phallus to that height from which it might seek transcendence. And sexual transcendence, some ecstasy where he could lose his ego for a moment, and his sense of self and his will, was life to him – he could not live without sexual transcendence (NM, pp. 131–5).

> . . . Never had a male novelist written more intimately about women – heart, contradiction, and soul; never had a novelist loved them more, been so comfortable in the tides of their sentiment, and so ready to see them murdered. His work held, on

the consequence, huge fascination for women . . . Indeed, which case-hardened guerrilla of Women's Liberation might not shed a private tear at the following passage: 'And if you're in Scotland and I'm in the Midlands, and I can't put my arms round you, and wrap my legs round you, yet I've got something of you . . . We fucked a flame into being. Even the flowers are fucked into being between the sun and the earth . . .' Yes, which stout partisan of the Liberation would reach such words and not go soft for the memory of some bitter bridge of love they had burned behind? (NM, pp. 134–5).

3 Women

Lawrence was obviously affected by the women he met in his own life: whether it was his mother, Jessie Chambers, Louie Burrows, Helen Corke, more crucially Alice Dax, or ultimately Frieda von Richtofen and her sisters. The comments about these women in his letters give interesting clues to his feelings about them. The depth of those feelings can only be realised from the women he portrayed in the novels. Nonetheless, the fictional women did not come out of thin air. They are a composite of his own ideas, the ideas of the times, and the expression of those ideas as lived by real women he loved.

It was in women that the young Lawrence saw people of his age struggling for liberation, defying social restrictions (SS, p. 47), anxious to lead a fuller life, attempting to escape in hope and imagination from the limiting social conditions. In his *Autobiographical Sketch*, he wrote:

> My mother's generation was the first generation of working class mothers to become really self-conscious, the woman freed herself at least mentally and spiritually from the husband's domination, and then she became that great institution, the character-forming power, the mother of my generation. I am sure the character of nine-tenths of the men of my generation was formed by the mother: the character of the daughters too (P, pp. 592–7).

The fact that he uses the phrase 'my mother's generation' shows how aware Lawrence was of social history and the forces at play in his own mother's life. As a young man, he expected a lot, too much, from the women he befriended. He wanted them to be his teachers, mentors and spiritual leaders. Often he was disappointed, which only ended in hurting the girl in question: Jessie Chambers and Louie Burrows were the notable ones whose pain has gone down in history. Like any idealist, Lawrence may have been searching for the perfect expression of his ideas in a woman, but he was not to be daunted if he did not find them. He invented them.

Helen Corke was a formidable woman whom Lawrence met in London, around the same time as he knew Louie Burrows. She was stronger than him, too strong, and not in mind for the kind of man–woman relationship he wanted. It was back in Eastwood that he met the first woman, after Louie, to give him an intellectual lead, who was of course Alice Dax, about whom he has unfortunately kept quiet. He had begun writing novels by this time. *The White Peacock* was completed, *Sons and Lovers* was started.

But when Lawrence met Frieda Weekly, and fell in love with this woman who personified his ideals, the transformation really began. He began rewriting *Sons and Lovers* four months after their elopement. Frieda herself does not appear in *Sons and Lovers*, except in as much as Frieda appears in all his novels. She was his idea. She talked; Lawrence listened and drank it all in. They fought, they argued, they lived and plunged to the depths and heights of life. Lawrence felt real at last. This was the ideal he'd had all along for life, why he had not been able to make a go of his relationships with Jessie or with Louie. And why should he have? By the time he came to devising his master plan for the two novels which he called *The Sisters*, Frieda was a more real person in terms of character for a novel. Frieda, herself, determined to be kept in the story in her own way, has written of *The Rainbow* that although Louie Burrows may have been in some part the model for Ursula, 'the inner relationship is Lawrence's and mine, like the ring scene in *Women in Love*, where I throw the ring at him' (PL, p. 287).

It is in Lawrence's own comments on Frieda, though, that we realise the strength of his feelings for this woman. In his *Letter*, dated 17 April 1912, he wrote,

She is ripping – she's the finest woman I've ever met – you must above all things meet her . . . she is the daughter of Baron von Richtofen, of the ancient and famous house of Richtofen – but she's splendid, she is really . . . Mrs —— is perfectly unconventional, but really good – in the best sense . . . Oh, but she is the woman of a lifetime.

Which she was indeed. On 9 May, he was writing, about their elopement and the reality of the relationship,

Oh Lord, what a mess to be in – and this after eight weeks of acquaintance! But I don't care a damn what it all costs . . . The Richtofens are an astonishing family – three girls – women – the eldest a Doctor of Social Economics – a Professor too – then Frieda – then the youngest – 28 – very beautiful rather splendid in her deliberate worldliness. They are a rare family – father a fierce old aristocrat – mother utterly non-moral, very kind.

Note the excitement in that letter; the thrill he feels at meeting this family of extraordinary women.

By the autumn of 1912, he was able to write to his old friend Edward Garnett, commenting on Garnett's play about Jeanne d'Arc, some of Lawrence's now crystallised views on women.

You cared for women not so much for what they were themselves as for what their men saw in them. So that after all in your work women seem not to have an existence, save that they are the projections of the men. That is, they seem almost entirely sexual answers to or discords with the men . . . They have each got an internal form, an internal self which remains firm and individual whatever love they may be subject to. It's the positivity of women you seem to deny – make them sort of instrumental. There is in Women such a big sufficiency unto themselves, more than in men.

That letter was written by a man who, until recently, had used women as an idea, and who was learning to see women as people beyond the idea. Also, it is a letter written by a man who, more than any other, had thought about women, worked out what it is he so admired in them, and was prepared to say so to his male friends – even though the opinion was unlikely to bring him much male approval. During this early period of his life with Frieda, we can feel the build up of his conviction that he was right in his attitude to women. On 23 December, he writes to Sallie Hopkin, 'I shall do a novel about Love Triumphant one day. I shall do my work for women, better than the suffrage'. In another letter, 'I'll do my life work, sticking up for the love between man and woman . . . I shall always be a priest of love, and now a glad one'. Frieda has said, acknowledging her own powers (though as the partner in the tempestuous relationship she was probably the last one to know it), 'Do you know how much liberating I did for Lawrence . . . It was given to me to make him flower'. She was right in that.

Despite their fights, which sometimes weakened and exhausted him, Lawrence once said in defence of Frieda to a friend, 'You don't know that a woman is not a man with a different sex. She is a different world'. He wrote a delicate letter to Ernest Weekly, which was printed in the papers as part of the divorce proceedings, in October 1913. It was sensitive to Weekly himself and showed Lawrence's understanding of Frieda, and of all women:

> Mrs Weekly is afraid of being stunted and not allowed to grow, so she must live her own life. Women in their natures are like giantesses; they will break through everything and go on with their own lives . . . in this hour we are only single men . . . Mrs Weekly must live largely and abundantly; it is her nature. To me it means the future. I feel as if my effort to live was all for her. Cannot we all forgive something?

It was, of course, a letter from the man on the winning side who can afford to sound generous, but in some of his phrases about Frieda's own nature, 'is afraid of being stunted and not allowed to grow, so she must live her own life', are themes that reappear so often through his fictional women.

A letter of April 1914 describes *The Sisters* again as a novel about 'becoming individual, self-responsible, taking her initiative' – the idea discussed in the previous chapter. Obviously, Lawrence had to defend himself sometimes, to his friends, for his ideas on women did not fit the view of their own world of what women were like. This view of the importance of women, and things feminine, came from idealism, or was in Lawrence's head only. As the century progressed many other people adopted similar views, yet Lawrence knew it was there in the women around him. It took a Lawrence to spot it as a movement real and deep-rooted, something important. He wrote in November 1917, to Cecil Gray:

> As for me and my 'women' – [presumably in defence of himself, and a slur on his 'women'] I know what they are and aren't, and though there is a certain messiness, there is a further reality . . . It means to me there is a whole world of knowledge to forsake, a new, deeper, lower one to *entamer* . . . my 'women' represent, in an impure and unproved, subservient, cringing, bad fashion, I admit but represent nonetheless the threshold of a new world, or

underworld, of knowledge and being . . . You want an emotional sensuous underworld, like Frieda and the Hebrideans: my 'women' want an ecstatic subtly-intellectual underworld, like the Greek-Orphicism – like Magdalene at her feet washing – and there you are.

I want to come now, in this chapter, to what I consider to be the central consideration of Lawrence and women. The women characters in his novels are so numerous, so vivid, so real, imaginative, complex and colourful, that there is no avoiding them. I cannot understand how Lawrence has been misjudged as a man who does not like women. It would be hard to devote your life to women and not like them. Lawrence's women are not men in women's clothing (his men are more like women in men's clothing). If you look at the list of women characters that follows, you will notice that nowhere in the novels do men get the same treatment. There are no men characters he builds, and creates, so lovingly; no men characters get the same in-depth treatment. Rupert Birkin, for example, who is so often cited as Lawrence/Birkin, is only an idea. We never see inside Birkin, what he is thinking, and feeling. It was because of these women characters that I myself began to love Lawrence, the novelist; after all, I kept finding myself there upon the pages. Here were real women, acting out lives of fifty years ago, but with the same feelings, motives and complexities of women of our generation. Nowhere before had I read such a brilliant summing-up of the claustrophobia women can feel about social limitations in their lives; or of the fears they feel when they step outside those limitations; or the paradox of the fight for freedom and fear of taking it up totally. These, then, are Lawrence's women.

LETTIE

The White Peacock was Lawrence's first novel, which he began writing in 1906 while he was taking his teaching certificate at Nottingham University. It is the novel that he was able to show his mother, as an advance copy from the publishers, on her deathbed just before its actual publication in 1911. Compared to his other novels, it is clumsily constructed. The first-person narration is an awkward device that leaves author and narrator Cyril in some ludicrous situations wondering how he can report on such and such a scene without being there. Poor Cyril ends up snooping in on many a lovers' walk between Lettie and George.

There is, in *The White Peacock*, the friendship between Cyril and George, a theme which Lawrence develops later in life. But still, the most important character and the one he obviously loves most, is Lettie, the peacock herself, who struts, flirts and falls to her own doom. Lettie's doom is not, however, like George's, so much of her own character and personality. George becomes a depressive, is morose, and turns to drink. Lettie becomes trapped in the traditional role of wife and mother, beautiful wife of a rich man at that, in which she dies a living death. It is rather a Hardyesque type of novel, heavy on the social realism of country life. But Lettie is interesting as one of his women characters, visualised before his ideas were sharpened by knowledge of Frieda.

Lettie is wilful, selfish, provocative – but Lawrence obviously likes her. 'She, who had always been so rippling in thoughtless life, sat down in the window sill to think, and her strong teeth bit at her handkerchief till it was torn in holes . . . She read all the things that dealt with modern woman' (WP, p. 92). Lettie already is suffering her fate. She has married Leslie through not having the strength of her desires to choose George whom she loves. George would not have been a socially acceptable match. Already, because of Lawrence's friendship with Jessie Chambers, he was aware that women read the books coming out on modern women. Why was Lettie doing that? Because she wanted to get out but did not know how to. As she says to Emily, George's sister (a 'nice girl' and perhaps an early model of Jessie), when they see a woman at the Kennells driven to baby battering,

'Ah, it's always the woman bears the burden,' said Lettie bitterly.
'If he'd helped her — wouldn't she have been a fine woman now – splendid? But she's dragged to bits. Men are brutes – marriage just gives scope to them', said Emily (WP, p. 160).

Lettie became engaged at 21 to Leslie, and she has a party to show off her ring; always a haughty girl, she wanted others to be envious. Lettie had grown up believing she could always have all she wanted. She still wanted George and was not prepared to face the tragedy of the real situation, which was that she could no longer command his affections. At the party, she enjoys taunting and teasing him still,

> 'And you?' she said, turning to him who was silent.
> 'What do you want me to say?' he asked
> 'Say what you like.'
> 'Sometime, when I've thought about it.'
> 'Cold dinners!' laughed Lettie, awaking Alice's old sarcasm at
> his slowness.
> 'What?' he exclaimed, looking up suddenly at her taunt. She
> knew she was playing false; she put the ring on her finger and
> went across the room to Leslie, laying her arm over his shoulder,
> and leaning her head against him, murmuring softly to him. He,
> poor fellow,was delighted with her, for she did not display her
> fondness often (WP, p. 135).

Lawrence's dialogue and scenes in this novel are some of the most
realistic in any of his writing. After *The White Peacock*, and perhaps
Sons and Lovers, he turned his path from that of social realism to
novels that would point his themes, his burning idea. These early
novels are to be enjoyed for a different Lawrence – the Lawrence
who is almost a playwright. The scenes are sharp, brightly painted,
and tense with feeling.

Lettie dances a mazurka with George. Now she is engaged, she
can play with him more viciously.

> 'You are different tonight', she said, leaning on him.
> 'Am I?' he replied 'It's because things are altered too. They're
> settled one way now – for the present at least.'
> 'Don't forget the two steps this time', said she, smiling, and
> adding seriously, 'You see, I couldn't help it.'
> 'No, why not?'
> 'Things! I have been brought up to expect it – everybody
> expected it – and you're bound to do what people expect you to do
> – you can't help it. We can't help ourselves, we're all chessmen',
> she said.
> 'Ay', he agreed, but doubtfully.
> 'I wonder where it will end', she said.
> 'Lettie!' he cried, and his hand closed in a grip on hers.
> 'Don't – don't say anything – it's no good now, it's too late. It's
> done and what is done, is done. If you talk any more, I shall say
> I'm tired and stop the dance. 'Don't say another word' (WP, p.
> 143).

Lawrence, writing this novel, was himself young, his own preoccupations were with getting married, with finding the right woman for life and love; he knew the dangers that lay before him, of marrying the wrong person. Anyone growing up in a small town or country area, knows what pressures are around as people get engaged and married off. What tragedies are writ in those smiling faces and optimistic smiles as the engagement and wedding rings are flashed around. *The White Peacock* is a novel that deserves a wider readership.

What was Lettie to do, now a lady married to Leslie, who was dull and gave her no emotional or spiritual feedback? Lettie is like a precursor of Connie – only not such a happy one. Somewhere, she hopes she can always have some pull over George. Perhaps they can have an affair? But social customs in those parts do not allow for that. Perhaps they could run away? Who, Lettie? Too much to lose again. 'She was at the bottom a seething confusion of emotion, and she wanted to make him likewise' (WP, p. 242). Lettie and George go for a walk, like old times, in the woods. The pastoral scene, the air laden with sexual promise, is very like the scenes Lawrence was to perfect at the end of his writing life, in *Lady Chatterley's Lover*. But here the emotions are, if anything, more clearly spelled out.

> She continued to look at him, and to smile. He said nothing. So they went on to where they could climb the fence into the spinney. She climbed to the top rail, holding by an oak bough. Then she let him lift her down bodily. 'Ah!', she said, 'you like to show me how strong you are – a veritable Samson!' – she mocked, although she had invited him with her eyes to take her in his arms . . . With her whimsical moods she tormented him.
> 'If we were trees with ivy – instead of being fine humans with free active life – we should hug our thinning lives, shouldn't we?'
> 'I suppose we should.'
> . . . She was too swift for him (WP, p. 242).

Lettie and George weep and try again to work out where they went wrong. Some of their love scenes are the tenderest and most excrutiating anywhere. But the reality sets in. Cyril explains some of what happens to Lettie. This is Lawrence projecting, on a young woman of his day, the same fate that beset the women of his mother's generation, if they did not manage to get out. He is quite clear in his views on what a waste it all is of a woman's potential:

Having reached that point in a woman's career when most, perhaps all of the things in life seem worthless and insipid, she had determined to put up with it, to ignore her own self, to empty her own potentialities into the vessel of another or others, and to live her life at second hand. This peculiar abnegation of self is the resource of a woman for the escaping of the responsibilities of her own development. Like a nun, she puts over her living face a veil, as a sign that the woman no longer exists for herself: she is the servant of God, of some man, of her children, or maybe of some cause . . . (WP, p. 323).

We recall that Lawrence, in those heady days of his years with Frieda, when his ideas began to make sense, wrote of his plan for *The Sisters* that it was to be a novel about 'woman becoming individual, self-responsible, taking her initiative'. This was the tragedy that Lawrence was wise enough to see, before the contemporary explosion in ideas about women needing to find themselves in life, not just through a man or children; finding their own direction, and form of self-expression. Lettie is his warning to young women. He knows how hard the path out there on one's own is going to be for women: to force themselves to be outcasts. For it is the same path Lawrence has to tread, to drag himself away from his background in the attempt to become as a young man, an artist. Cyril's words continued, 'To be responsible for the good progress of one's life is terrifying. It is the most insufferable form of loneliness, and the heaviest of responsibilities. So Lettie indulged her husband, but did not yield her independence to him . . .' (WP, p. 324)

Lawrence's Lettie, in fact, cracked open the hollow shell of the feminine mystique long before post-Second World War women did, when she expressed her feelings about being a mother and housewife:

'I hope I shall have another child next spring', she would write, 'there is only that to take away the misery of this torpor. I seem full of passion and energy, and it all fizzles out in day-to-day domestics.'

[Cyril] When I replied to her urging her to take some work that she could throw her soul into, she would reply indifferently . . .

Like so many women, she seemed to live, for the most part contentedly, a small indoor existence with artifical light and padded upholstery. Only occasionally, hearing the winds of life outside, she clamoured to be out in the black, keen storm. She was driven to the door, she looked out and called into the tumult wildly, but feminine caution kept her from stepping over the threshold (WP, pp. 330–1).

Mrs Morel

Sons and Lovers was Lawrence's expurgation of all the passion of his youth and growing up. As such, it is one of the most intense portrayals of adolescent life; the teenage of a young man; playing with sex; the need for communion with a girl; love of the first woman he has known, his mother; moving from girl to girl; trying to understand the explosive feelings bottled up inside him. I do not take Paul Morel as a particular case of the Freudian complexes. Lawrence may have heard about Freud from Frieda but that would not have changed the whole direction of the novel, just given him strength in its direction. I do not want to go into the character of Paul, nor the relationship between him and his mother, so much as to show the characterisation of the women the novel involves. They, as always, are to me the interesting part.

The mother, Gertrude Morel, is well known as the thwarted, frustrated young woman, of middle-class origin, who fell for a miner because he danced well, married him and lived to regret her marriage and life, in the dull tenements of Nottinghamshire collieries, and the poverty-stricken, argumentative family life that became her lot. As indicated before, Lawrence was aware not only of his mother's aspirations for her sons, but also of her aspirations for herself. Lawrence puts in the small but important bits of her life, which show her mind trying to grapple with her reality, and her own attempts to get out and beyond. 'She loved ideas', he wrote, 'and was considered very intellectual . . . She was to the miner that thing of mystery and fascination, a lady' (SL, p. 17). Mrs Morel joined the Women's Guild,

Sometimes Mrs Morel read a paper. It seemed queer to the children to see their mother, who was always busy about the house, sitting writing in her rapid fashion, thinking, referring to books, and writing again . . . The Guild was called by some hostile husbands, who found their wives getting too independent, the 'clat-fart' shop – that is, the gossip shop . . . the women could look at their homes, at the conditions of their own lives, and find fault (SL, p. 68).

That is enough of an indication that Lawrence knew what his own mother, and Mrs Morel, were feeling all along.

MIRIAM

Miriam, modelled so exclusively on Jessie Chambers, a portrayal that the real Jessie did not like, seems to have had rather a poor press on the whole. Despite the fact that Miriam was the girl Paul Morel treated quite cruelly, the girl to whom he spoke sharply about her not enjoying sex, and his wanting to communicate with, but not kiss her, Miriam nevertheless comes over as a strong female character. She was not just the dreamy girl, who liked looking at flowers and reading books. Aside from her relationship with Paul Morel, she was also a thinking, feeling girl of her own time, who did not happen to be the right girl in the end for Paul/Lawrence.

In Miriam, Lawrence was describing for the first time the kind of female he found guiding and leading him. Whatever he wrote about her, he felt himself. 'She wanted to be considered. She wanted to learn, thinking that if she could read . . . the world would have a different face for her and a deepened respect . . . She must have something to reinforce her pride, because she felt different from other people . . . On the whole, she scorned the male sex' (SL, p. 178).

Miriam grew up on the farm that Lawrence so idealised but still the writer was sharp enough to detect her own dissatisfaction with that way of life. She did not like her lot, as a girl. 'I'm all day cleaning what the boys make just as bad in five minutes. I don't *want* to be at home . . . I want to do something. I want a chance like anybody else. Why should I, because I'm a girl, be kept at home and not allowed to be anything?' (SL, p. 191). In fact, much of the generally accepted view of Miriam is a mistaken one, because it is Paul's interpretation of her: and as such that of the young man trying to come to terms with a young woman, not this time his own projection, but a person in her own right. When Paul wonders why Miriam wishes she were a man, but seems to hate men at the same time, it is his inability to comprehend that, not ours. Of course she hates men. She is surrounded by men who hold her down: brothers she has to clean up after, a father who cannot see there might be more to her life. 'Why *shouldn't* I know mathematics? Yes!' she cried, her eyes expanding in a kind of defiance (SL, p. 192). Poor Miriam had an almost unequal battle on her hands. As for her famous sentiments, that show her to be sexually sterile, Miriam can be seen simply as a girl trying to come to terms with female sexuality. She wanted more in life than marriage and motherhood, and so sex had become equated to her with pregnancy. Hence, she looks at the mare in horror and cannot bear the thought of the mare's life. Paul sees it as a denial of sexuality, that she won't give in. Another woman could understand what Miriam felt: 'It could never be mentioned that the mare was in foal' (SL, p. 201).

Miriam does suffer. She is not built up completely as a character and we tend to see the unfinished, rather bitter side of her. She was actually further ahead, in her growing up, than Paul. Later, when Paul is involved with Clara Dawes, the girl says to Paul: 'It's so unjust . . . the man does as he likes . . .'. She is referring to the gossip about Clara, who has left her husband and is now living as a married woman on her own. Miriam sees the social injustice, if Paul does not. He is still a crass young man, wondering why women do not get on with things, instead of grumbling. Miriam knows why.

'Then let the woman also', he said.
'How can she? And if she does, look at her position.'
'What of it?'
'Why it's impossible! You don't understand what a woman forfeits' (SL, p. 385).

Lawrence had by then met Alice Dax and Frieda, both of whom had risked all social conformity by having affairs as married women. He knew it was not easy. Paul, however, is selfishly drawn as a young man pursuing his own growth and development, not in the least understanding of what Miriam may be feeling. When, later in the novel, she tells him she is going to the farming college at Broughton for three months, to train, perhaps to teach, he says, 'I say – that sounds all right for you! You always wanted to be independent' (SL, p. 504). Lawrence is exposing Paul here more than Miriam, for lack of perception. For Paul continues, reflectively, still picking up on the ideas of his father's generation of men, 'I suppose work *can* be nearly everything to a man', he said, 'though it isn't to me. But a woman only works with a part of herself. The real and vital part is covered up'.

'But a man can give *all* himself to a work? . . . And a woman only
the unimportant part of herself? . . . Then . . . if it's true, it's great
shame' (SL, p. 505). Miriam speaks those words, her eyes dilated
with anger.

CLARA DAWES

Clara is Paul's next sexual, or rather romantic excursion. It is from
Clara he learns the excitement of sensuality in woman, and that a
woman can be as definite as a man about wanting sex. Clara was
perhaps modelled on Alice Dax, and partly on Frieda. She is an
interesting character, showing us the kind of world Lawrence had
already mingled in, and noticed. The women he knew were thinking people, perhaps intellectual, who were caught up in the
Suffragette movement. Paul/Lawrence was rather two-minded
about it, as any man might have been. Lawrence basically
understood women's needs to express themselves. He just did not
like their demanding the vote in that single-minded fashion. To
him, there was more at stake for women to sort out. But Paul is
interested in Clara, in the same way as Lawrence was presumably
interested in Alice Dax. This type of woman was a teacher to him as
she was already striding ahead: 'Mrs Dawes was separated from her
husband, and had taken up Women's Rights. She was supposed to
be clever. It interested Paul' (SL, p. 229). He was also sexually
attracted to her. So, despite his protestations to Miriam, he was not
simply attracted to the sensuous woman, the whore type, but to the
type of woman who had worked out her own place in the world, and
was able to express her own sexuality. He needed that, as would any
man.

Paul has a lot to learn from Clara. So many times, in *Sons and
Lovers*, Paul lets himself be lectured by his various women. It is
Lawrence's way of getting over new ideas. He has not yet reached
the state where, as the author, he can recite them with authority.
Nor can he in all honesty put them in the mouths of the male
characters. This is the young man's journey, his adventure in
learning about life. He learns from women. Clara has to defend
Margaret Bonford, to Paul's scorn; a Suffragette,

'It's not heaven she wants to get – it's her fair share on earth',
retorted Clara . . .

'Well,' he said. 'I thought she was warm, and awfully nice –
only too frail. I wished she was sitting comfortably in peace . . .'
  'Darning her husband's stockings', said Clara scathingly (SL, p.
283).

Many critics have declared that Lawrence hated the character Clara,
but I do not see that at all. He sets himself up, as Paul, to be knocked
down by her. The conversation is realistic, and goes on between
many young men and women. Paul makes the obvious male statement that the woman seems to be making herself unhappy with all
this suffragettism, and Clara points out that Paul thinks she'd be
happier darning her husband's stockings. Change takes time, effort
and pain.
  Clara has some tough lines, but then she has chosen a fairly tough
path in life. It is not easy to live as a separated woman. Mrs Leivers
disapproves of her. She says, to Clara, though probably enviously,

  'And you find life happier now?'
  'Infinitely.'
  'And are you satisfied?'
  'So long as I can be free and independent' (SL, p. 285).

  Like Miriam, Clara is rather down on men, and caustic in her new
found feminist ideas. She works 'jennying' in a mill. 'Is it sweated?'
'More or less. Isn't *all* women's work? That's another trick the men
have played, since we forced ourselves into the labour market' (SL,
p. 320). The lines may read rather false, but are exactly the kind of
words a young woman, fresh from political meetings and dis-
cussions, voices. Lawrence knew it all well, from the meetings at
Eastwood. Again of Clara, he writes, 'During the ten years that she
had belonged to the women's movement she had acquired a fair
amount of education . . . She considered herself as a woman apart,
and particularly apart, from her class' (SL, p. 323). In that way, he
excuses her much. She is not flirting with the ideas. She has been
part of the women's movement for ten years. Alice Dax had to be the
formidable model.
  Clara also lectures Paul on his attitude towards women, for she
knows how a girl like Miriam must have suffered at his selfish
hands. When Paul is explaining to Clara about Miriam, about what
went wrong, he says, '[She] Wants the soul out of my body'. Clara
asks him how long they had been going together. He says, seven

years. Clara's retort: 'And you haven't found out the very first thing about her . . . That she doesn't want any of your soul communion. That's your own imagination. She wants you . . .' (SL, p. 339). Good for Clara. Miriam did want Paul. But she dare not give herself totally, until she felt some commitment from him. She was not as brave as Clara, nor as old. Clara and Miriam also became friends, defending each other both to Paul and to Mrs Morel – just as Jessie Chambers and Alice Dax supported each other.

THE BRANGWEN WOMEN

Thus to *The Rainbow*, and the first novel in the work Lawrence called *The Sisters*. This was the work inspired by his knowledge of Frieda, by the realisation of his feelings about women, and his desire really to explore what the adventure would be of the individual woman, taking responsibility for her own life. The first few pages in which he describes the Brangwen women, as a dynasty, are remnants of the previous novels, a tying up of the ends of his old ideas. They are crucial paragraphs, that link his feelings about women, about nature and life, and what it is that the women's struggle is all about. It is at this point that feminist critics have become unsure of Lawrence, because he seems to be saying that women can free themselves, but have to stick with what nature ordains. These ideas are part of Lawrence's more complicated philosophy of duality: the underlying force between any man/woman, society/nature relationship, which I shall explain in depth later. Martin Green sums up what Lawrence wanted from women:

> . . . he did not want to show [women] finding fulfillment in the world of men. Ursula was to be Frieda . . . she was to go into and through the world of men, but out the other side, into a higher form of what I have called the world of Women. There, ideally, she would achieve a life so splendid that it would compel men also into admiring emulation, and so, to some degree, save the world just as much as suffrage claimed it was going to (MG, p. 343).

For, as has been said earlier, Lawrence did not like the world of men. He wanted a change, to the feminisation of ideas. For now, however, the Brangwen women and what they symbolised to Lawrence:

The women were different. On them too was the drowse of blood-intimacy . . . But the women looked out from the heated, blind intercourse of farm-life, to the spoken world beyond. They were aware of the lips and the mind of the world speaking and giving utterance, they heard the sound in the distance, and they strained to listen.

. . . But the woman wanted another form of life than this, something that was not blood-intimacy . . . the world beyond. She stood to see the far-off world of cities and governments and the active scope of man, the magic land to her, where secrets were made known and desires fulfilled. She faced outwards to where men moved dominant and creative, having turned their back on the pulsating heart of creation, and with this behind them, were set out to discover what was beyond, to enlarge their own scope and range and freedom; whereas the Brangwen men faced inwards to the teeming life of creation, which poured unresolved into their veins (R, pp. 8–9).

LYDIA

Lydia Brangwen, the grandmother of Ursula, is a rather shadowy figure, the Polish woman with a little daughter whom Tom Brangwen courts and marries. She brings her foreignness, its blood and mysteries to life in Nottinghamshire – and her past. Strong, obdurate and silent, she is sometimes drawn resembling Lawrence's own mother, or Mrs Morel, the already middle-aged woman who wants something better for her children. 'She craved to know. She craved to achieve this higher being, if not in herself, then in her children . . . She decided it was a question of knowledge' (R, p. 10). Like Lawrence's own mother, she saw the way out through education; to get her children out of their class, enable them to move, journey, explore. Lydia, with Tom, first shows that awful Brangwen womanpower, that is to increase with Anna and Ursula. Lydia does not dominate Tom, but she certainly shows him the way she expects to be treated. The lead comes from her. 'She waited for him to meet her, not to bow before her and serve her.' For Lydia had already learned from her former marriage to Lensky, the Pole, what male dominance meant. 'He incorporated her in his ideas, as if she were not a person herself, as if she were just his aide-de-camp . . .

gradually at twenty-three, twenty-four, she began to realise that she too might consider these ideas . . . His then, was not the only male mind' (R, pp. 256–7). It is Lydia Lensky we see in the next but one generation – in Ursula.

ANNA

The portrait of Anna is lovely and skilful. With Anna, we begin to see the Lawrence magic and fine touch with his women characters. Anna is whole, and she is real. As a little girl, she likes to go with her father, Tom, and enjoys the outside male world. His friends laugh at her as a 'polecat'. She is fiery and knows her own mind. At eighteen, she is a headstrong young woman, with ideals and a sense of where she is going. Already, she knows the very real danger of claustrophobia, of being trapped in small communities like their own. Anna wants more. She is horrified by stories of torture cells. Like any adolescent girl, Anna has her models she looks up to, as a way of defining what sort of life she wants. She is described as something of a snob, because she does not want to be ordinary. The ladies in pictures who intrigued her were such as Alexandra, Princess of Wales 'This lady was proud and royal, and stepped indifferently over all the small, mean desires' (R, p. 102). For Anna wants to be 'a proud, free lady absolved from the petty ties, existing beyond petty considerations'.

But Anna's generation has not the means of escape. She is still too much like Lettie to know where the way out lies. She meets Will and starts to exercise her energies over him. Anna and Will marry very young. Their relationship is a vivid portrait of the battle that goes on between two young people playing at love and marriage with very little experience behind them. The relationship will be discussed later. Throughout, though, we see Anna's spirit. Not Will, poor Will. He again is a mere shadow.

Anna can be haughty with Will, when she is feeling strong and superior. She comes out with the new ideas too: 'Respect what?' she asked . . . 'It is impudence to say that Woman was made out of Man's body', she continued, 'when every man is born of woman. What impudence men have, what arrogance' (R, p. 174). Anna's will is shown as strong, but directionless. She is wilful and provocative, rather like Lettie. When Will fancies other women, Anna expresses her independence. She would have her own adventures. She felt liberated – not the dull housewife image for her. 'She challenged him, with a sort of radiance, very bright and free, opposite to him.' But Anna soon retreats. She begins to have children – the one side of female life Lawrence never goes into is women with children, he neither knew it nor cared for it, as with Frieda and her own children – and gives up the struggle facing women. Anna does not feel like embarking on new ground, 'There was something beyond her. But why must she start on the journey? . . . soon again she was with child . . . through her another soul was coming, to stand upon her as upon the threshold looking out, shading its eyes for the direction to take' (R, pp. 195–6).

URSULA

Ursula is the path, the direction. Ursula is Lawrence's woman who becomes self-responsible, who takes the journey that Lawrence himself has to take. She is the central character in all his work. Lawrence does not hide the fact either. He describes her type of independence:

> She knew that soon she would want to become a self-responsible person . . . An all-containing will in her for complete independence, complete social independence, complete independence from any personal authority, kept her dullishly at her studies . . . she knew that she had always her price of ransom – her femaleness . . . There was the mysterious man's world to be adventured upon, the world of daily work and duty, and existence as a working member of the community . . . She wanted to make her conquest also of this man's world (R, p. 334).

In Ursula, we sense the excitement of a real change in the history of women. Now education, and the social milieu, were ready to accept them – these free young women – Ursula was going to study, train and get out there into the man's world. She wanted to know what a job, what being out there, was all about. She also wanted to know about love. Ursula rejected her mother's way of life. 'When she saw, later, a Rubens picture with storms of naked babies, and found this was called "Fecundity", she shuddered and the word became abhorrent to her . . . as a child she was against her mother . . . she craved for some spirituality and stateliness' (R, p. 264).

What makes Ursula even more unique, as a feminine character in literature, is that Lawrence in his attempt to show her as a fully independent-minded and very passionate young woman, gives her a teenage homosexual love for her teacher Winifred Inger. Winifred Inger has angered feminist critics because Lawrence implies that she is not a happy woman; as though he were saying no lesbian could be happy. Lawrence may well have believed that. But then, also, it is not hard to imagine that even in the 1910s it was not easy to live as a lesbian and feel fully content. More interesting, is that Ursula was inspired by this woman. She represented something to the teenage girl, intent on finding her full independence. Winifred is described thus: 'a rather beautiful woman of twenty-eight, a fearless-seeming clean type of modern girl whose very independence betrays her sorrow . . . Ursula felt her whole life begin when Miss Inger came into the room . . . what Ursula adored so much was her fine, upright, athletic bearing, and her indomitably proud nature. She was proud and free as a man, yet exquisite as a woman' (R, pp. 336–7). What was important to Ursula was how to attain the pride and freedom of a man, with the essential beauty that still lies in being a woman. Through Miss Inger, Ursula learns to be wary of submissiveness. Miss Inger draws for her the image of the lion and the eagle:

> She did not see how lambs could love. Lambs could only be loved. They could only be afraid, and tremblingly submit to fear, and become sacrificial; or they could submit to love, and become beloveds. In both they were passive . . . her own limbs like a lion or a wild horse, her heart was relentless in its desires (R, p. 342).

Earlier, as a seventeen-year-old, in her new relationship with the young Skrebensky, Ursula has shown some of that fire. She is getting ready to define herself sexually: 'A sort of defiance of all the world possessed her in it – she would kiss him just because she wanted to' (R, p. 302). Ursula is quite a fighter.

As Ursula grows up and studies for exams to become a teacher – this is Lawrence's career also, the same path taken by him – what happens to her mirrors what was happening in the history of the world around her. Miss Inger has been involved in the women's movement. Ursula brings the arguments home, on the rights of women to take equal place with men in the outside world of work. Lawrence even gives one of her teachers a speech to say that economic independence is much more important than it seems. The teacher knows that it is only by being financially independent that any of the girls will really be able to have the freedom to choose her own way of life. Ursula applies to a school in Kingston, and dreams of getting away from home. Her father refuses permission. Both her parents feel threatened by Ursula's actions. She goes to teach instead at Ilkeston, similarly to Lawrence's experience of teaching in a Nottinghamshire miners' school, with all the horrors of it. There, however, she meets Maggie Schofield, who teaches her not to be made depressed or miserable by the school, and the petty cruel-minded, unfeeling world.

Maggie shows Ursula a new world, introduces her to new ideas, such as feminism and vegetarianism. Maggie is one of the suffragettes and believes implicitly in the vote. Already, Ursula has a feeling of her own place in the new politics. Here we see more clearly Lawrence's attitude – that women must go beyond feminism to find a world that neither men nor women as yet knew about. They should not try to emulate the mess men had made of the world.

> For her, as for Maggie, the liberty of women meant something real and deep. She felt that somewhere, in something, she was not free. And she wanted to be . . . In coming out and earning her own living, she had made a strong, cruel move towards freeing herself. But having more freedom she only became profoundly aware of the big want (R, p. 406).

At this point, feminist critics have laughed at Lawrence, saying Ursula only wanted a man. In fact, Lawrence goes on to describe the 'big want'. It is everything lovely in ordinary life: the world of aestheticism, feelings, experiences and, yes, love: relationship with the opposite, with a man, which would lead her into ever yet more fascinating realms of experience. Not marriage of the traditional type, but something evolving. 'She wanted to read great, beautiful books, and be rich with them, she wanted to see beautiful things, and have the joy of them for ever; she wanted to know big, free people; and there remained always the want she could put no name to' (R, p. 406).

Ursula and Maggie go to suffragette meetings in Nottingham. They talk and read Shelley and Browning and a work about Women and Labour. They talk too, of love, marriage and the position of women in marriage. But, as Ursula grows up, leaves home, faces her financial independence, all the problems of adulthood crowd round. What sort of life should she choose? Is she really strong enough in the end to break free, wander into the isolated unknown, disappoint her parents? She meets Anthony, who offers marriage. Is this the way out after all the youthful idealism? Ursula is still strong enough to know her own mind: 'she was a traveller on the face of the earth, and she was an isolated creature living in the fulfilment of his own senses . . . ultimately and finally, she must go on and on, seeking the goal that she knew she did draw nearer to' (R, p. 417). It is a hard and lonely path she has chosen.

At college, Ursula makes another friend, Dorothy Russell, who again spends all her free time working for the Women's Social and Political Union. With exams over, Ursula is face to face with her own fate. Skrebensky is still around. 'It was for her to choose between being Mrs Skrebensky, even Baroness Skrebensky, wife of a lieutenant in the Royal Engineers, the Sappers, as he called them, living with the European population in India – or being Ursula Brangwen, spinster, schoolmistress' (R, p. 474). In 1920, imagine how much harder the choice was – since it can still be hard even today.

Ursula goes through all the problems of the modern young woman. She chooses to be sexually independent, not to marry, then she thinks she might be pregnant by Skrebensky. Again, she worries 'Was it not enough that she had her man, her children, her place of shelter under the sun? Was it not enough for her, as it had been for her mother?' (R, p. 485). She even views the idea of being a single mother: which shows how far she has come from the position of Lettie or Anna. After all, what had the child to do with him? 'Why must she be bound, aching and cramped with the bondage to Skrebensky and Skrebensky's world?' (R, p. 492). Lawrence gives the young modern woman every credence for fearing the trap he saw so many wasted by. But Ursula can still see her way out. She is not pregnant, and so the question of what she would have done, in those days, is not answered, but she repeats to herself, 'I have no father, nor mother nor lover, I have no allocated place in the world of things, I do not belong to Beldover nor to Nottingham nor to England nor to this world, they none of them exist, I am trammelled and entangled in them, but they are all unreal' (R, p. 493). Just, as one imagines, Lawrence must have had to reassure himself about his own sense of direction.

HERMIONE

Hermione Roddice, in *Women in Love*, the second part of Lawrence's work *The Sisters*, is often described as one of his most vitriolic attacks on women. Lady Ottoline Morrell, who recognised herself in the portrait, wrote to Lawrence in anger. Hermione really is little like the picture of Ottoline that has come down to us today. Ottoline was a much more interesting and varied character. Hermione, in this novel, is a minor character, who becomes something of a butt for Lawrence to show what kind of woman was really leading the way for him. Hermione: 'She was passionately interested in reform, her soul was given up to the public cause. But she was a man's woman, it was the manly world that held her . . . she was a *Kulturträger*, a medium for the culture of ideas' (WL, p. 17). Hermione has gone over the top, for change in woman's role. She believes only in man's things, 'she betrayed the woman in herself'. At this point in the novel, Lawrence is setting up a woman who will be fit mate and partner for Rupert Birkin; someone who will be able to explore the new world of relationships, where man and woman are striving for something unique and as yet undiscovered. Hermione was not enough. She had the independence of mind and spirit, but she had not held on to her femaleness, to make her sufficiently the 'other' to Birkin's male. Ursula's comment to Hermione is interesting. She says, 'It is you who want a physically strong, bullying man, not I. It is you who want an insensitive man, not I . . . You don't give him a woman's love, you give him an ideal love'. Ursula, however, figures little in the novel, other than as the partner to Birkin. It is Gudrun who grows more as a character – who takes on Ursula's mantle.

GUDRUN

Gudrun in *Women in Love* is Ursula's sister. They have both returned from school abroad, come back to Nottinghamshire, and are trying to face their futures. Is it to be marriage, career, or both? Gudrun explores the idea of a woman finding herself in a creative art, as an artist, more than Ursula ever has. She is more acerbic than Ursula, and has a sense of humour. The novels do not read on in sequel, but many similar themes are explored. Gudrun, for example, is already an independent woman, but sometimes she indulges in the fantasy that she is not – that she is the clinging, submissive type again. For instance, when she meets and is attracted to Gerald: 'to Gudrun it was a real delight, in make-belief, to be the childlike, clinging woman to the man who stood there on the quay, so good-looking and efficient in his white clothes . . .' (WL, p. 183). Romantic fantasy for her. She and Ursula talk a lot in the early part of the novel about their ideas on marriage. When Ursula rejects Birkin's marriage proposal – it seems too much as if he has chosen her to live out his ideal, his idea – Gudrun says, 'I think it would be too wearing, too exhausting. One would be shouted down every time, and rushed into his way without any choice. He would want to control you entirely. He cannot allow that there is any other mind than his own' (WL, p. 297). Ursula puts in one of her few bits of candour in this novel: 'The nuisance is . . . that one would find almost any man intolerable after a fortnight.'

Gudrun is trying to work out her own ideas. She is interested in free love, which was a relatively new concept in those days, discussed and explored on the edges of literary bohemia – a world of which the writer Lawrence was now much more a part. 'I'm sure a mistress is more likely to be faithful than a wife – just because she is her *own* mistress. No – he says he believes that a man and wife can go further than any other two beings – but *where* is not explained' (WL, p. 327). Gudrun's redefinition of 'mistress', as mistress of herself, is one that would please contemporary minds. Later, as Ursula gets more involved with Birkin, Gudrun excuses her sister's lapse, by saying that marriage to him would at least never be ordinary. 'But with the ordinary man, who has his life fixed in one place, marriage is just impossible . . . the very thought of it sends me *mad*' (WL, p. 422). Gudrun is ahead now of all Lawrence's other women. 'One must be free, above all, one must be free . . . No man will be sufficient to make that good – no man! To marry, one must have a free lance or nothing, a comrade-in-arms, a *Glücksritter* . . . I'd tilt the world with a *Glücksritter*. But a home, an establishment' (WL, p. 422). Ursula joins in, cynically imagining either of them in the clichéd 'little grey home in the west'. One senses one can hear Frieda in Gudrun's cries for freedom. It also strikes a true note for contemporary women – the fear of being held back by a man, being made to conform and become ordinary.

But where Lawrence scores with both Ursula and Gudrun is that he does not make them champions for their cause, braver than you or me. He shows them as being confused, often fearful, and tempted to backslide. Gudrun goes through a phase of wanting marriage, the stability of marriage. 'She did not want it, let her say what she might. She had been lying. The old idea of marriage was right even now – marriage and the home. Yet her mouth gave a little grimace at the words . . . perhaps it was not in her to marry. She was one of life's outcasts, one of the drifting lives that have no root' (WL, p. 424). Then Gudrun meets Loerke, also an artist, who brings out in her the confidence to go ahead and face the fact that she is different. As an artist, and a woman, she has an obligation to herself. Gudrun fantasises about other great women in the past, like Cleopatra, who just used men for what she needed from them, and then threw them aside.

Through Gudrun, Lawrence is able to ask the great Freudian question: What is it after all, that woman wanted? Gudrun has to face herself with many questions – does she just want to be a success, to fulfil her ambitions, to succeed in the man's world? Or does she want union, with a man, in love? With Loerke's encouragement, though, she is able to laugh at the pressures pulling her to be ordinary, 'In England it was chic to be perfectly ordinary'. While Ursula tries her experiment in loving with Birkin, Gudrun is continuing the fight for women finding what independence really means.

ALVINA

Alvina Houghton of *The Lost Girl* is another of Lawrence's striking young women. She is less well known than Ursula and Gudrun, but I find her story fascinating. *The Lost Girl* was begun in 1912, at the same time as Lawrence was writing *The Rainbow*. Although the first draft was ready by 1913, Lawrence and Frieda left the manuscript with Frieda's mother in Germany, when they left for Italy, and then, during the war years, could not get hold of it. Lawrence finally rewrote it to be published in 1920. We get a mixture of the ideas that motivated Ursula in *The Rainbow*, and the ideas of the later Lawrence – that women were not going to find what they were looking for in the dead menfolk of England. They, like him, had to leave the drab grey country and find the sun. Alvina finds her salvation in Cicio.

Alvina is the 'lost girl' because she, too, is wandering, exploring, an outcast. At one point, the old maid who is her guardian, as her mother has died, asks her about Cicio – the circus artist she has met and is going to run away with – whether she intends to get married.

'I don't know . . .'
'You're a lost girl,' cried Miss Pinnegar . . .
'I like being lost', said Alvina (LG, p. 260).

Alvina is a high-spirited, strong-willed girl, who shows up splendidly the awful social position of young women. Lawrence opens the novel on that note of social realism, depressing and grey though it is.

1913. A calm year of plenty. But one chronic and dreary malady: that of the odd women. Why, in the name of all prosperity, should every class but the lowest in such a society hang over-burdened with Dead Sea fruit of odd women, unmarried, unmarriageable women, called old maids? Why is it that every tradesman, every schoolteacher, every bank manager, and every clergyman produces one, two, three old maids . . . However it be, it is a tragedy. Or perhaps it is not.

Perhaps these unmarried women of the middle classes are the famous sexless-workers of our ant-industrial society, of which we hear so much. Perhaps all they lack is an occupation: in short, a job (LG, pp. 11–12).

Lawrence is being ironical, because he sees two causes in the tragedy. One is that the women were not allowed to get jobs, to prove themselves in some way. But the second, and much stronger, is that they had no chance to release their sexual energy and desires. They rejected the young men offered to them because they knew something was missing. Love, desire, sex, were missing in the men's attitude toward them, and their attitude towards the men.

Alvina finds out – the hard way. Alvina's spirit leads her to such dissatisfaction with her life in Manchester House, under the rule of her eccentric father and the two old maids who run the domestic side, that she knows she cannot stay there all her life. 'I'm buried alive – simply buried alive. And it's more than I can stand. It is, really,' she says, reiterating a Lawrentian theme for women. Alvina decides to take up a job, a profession: nursing was one way out. She goes to Islington, in London, to train for six months. And Lawrence points out the irony that her nurse's uniform replaced the trousseau her parents might have expected for their daughter's leaving home. 'Instead of a wreath of orange blossom, a rather chic nurse's bonnet of blue silk, and for a trailing veil, a blue silk fall' (LG, p. 44). Alvina experiences all sorts of freedoms away from home. She learns her power over young men, but she doesn't want to be tied down to one of them. She senses sexuality, but doesn't know even what it is. 'She liked their arm round her waist, the kisses as she reached back her face, straining away, the sometimes desperate struggles . . . A super-human, voltaic force filled her. For a moment she surged in massive, inhuman, female strength. The men always wilted' (LG, p. 52). The men like her, because she is not out to trap them into marriage like most girls. She wonders about the fact that she is still a virgin. She wishes she had had the courage to lose her virginity. But one can imagine how hard that must have been in those days. In the end, she is still on her own, and she has to go back to Manchester House, in the village of Woodhouse, 'virgin as she had left it'. At least, she hopes, as a trained midwife, she will be able to make a decent living delivering babies. 'She would be independent, she could laugh everyone in the face' (LG, p. 55). But it does not work. People did not have babies, and if they did, they did not want to pay Alvina for her services. Suddenly her prospects look bleak again. The only way out was going to be marriage after all.

When she is 26, penniless, feeling drab and shabby, she has a suitor, Albert, and her panic begins about dying an old maid like all the others. Alvina's panic is very recognisable, as she thinks, 'She would become loose, she would become a prostitute, she said to herself, rather than die off . . . wither slowly and ignominiously and hideously on the tree. She would rather kill herself' (LG, p. 81). Then the circus arrives, with the trapeze artistes, of whom Cicio is a one, and she is seduced by his dark eyes, and, although they can hardly speak to each other, the promise of sexuality, of something earthy and basic, is more than she could ever hope for in Woodhouse. Her courage in realising herself an outcast is nicely drawn.

Sitting on the top of the covered car . . . so obviously a dark-skinned foreigner. And Alvina, who sat beside him, was reminded of the woman with the negro husband, down in Lumley. She understood the woman's reserve. She herself felt, in the same way, something of an outcast, because of the man at her side. An outcast! And glad to be an outcast. She clung to Cicio's dark, despised foreign nature. She loved it, she worshipped it, she defied all the other world (LG, p. 258).

She was glad to reject her own people. 'I want to go into the sun', she said.

MISS FROST

The very real threat in Alvina's life is the figure of Miss Frost, a miserable, bitter woman, who lacked complete control over her own fate. Alvina is accused of not wanting to think of what happened to her mother. Miss Frost, however, brooded on the fate of the dead woman. 'Bitterly she brooded on the lot of woman. Here was Clariss Houghton, married, and a mother – and dead. What a life! Who was responsible? James Houghton' (LG, P. 59). Miss Frost suffers all the confusions of being a non-self-actuating person.

Yet why? Why was James more guilty than Clariss? Is the only aim and end of a man's life, to make some woman, or parcel of woman, happy? Why? Why should anyone expect to be *made happy*, and develop heart disease if she isn't? . . . Miss Frost wept in anguish, and saw nothing but another woman betrayed to sorrow and a slow death. Sorrow and a slow death because a man had married her. Miss Frost wept also for herself . . . because a man had *not* married her (LG, p. 16).

KATE LESLIE

The Plumed Serpent was published in 1926. It recounts much of Lawrence's own voyage of discovery for another, more meaningful life, than the one he found in the drab coal-mining districts of England. He had visited America, and Mexico. In this novel, he uses Kate, a woman of 40, facing other crises in her own life. Not for her the fears of spinsterdom, or dying a virgin. She has been married, twice, and has even experienced the great love of her life. She has children whom she has left behind, they are growing up in London and no longer need her. She is facing what we would now call her mid-life crisis. There is still something she wants in life. But what is it? Lawrence draws us into Kate in a very interesting way. Much of the novel is written in the contemporary vein of seeing Kate through her own continuous thoughts.

Kate is a widow, and lonely now. She married young, and her

grown-up children are 21 and 19. She had divorced their father ten years previously, and they stayed with him. She divorced him to marry James Joachim Leslie, a revolutionary, political man. But he is now dead. 'She had lived her life. She had had her lovers, her two husbands, her children.' She had loved Joachim as much as a woman can love a man, so she was no longer in love with love. She did not yearn for the love of a man, or even of her children. She yearned for companionship and sympathy, but what she did have now was peace. 'No, she no longer wanted love, excitement, and something to fill her life. She was forty, and in the rare, lingering dawn of her maturity, the flower of her soul was opening' (PS, pp. 65–6). This is Lawrence reaching maturity, too, of course.

Some signs are given of Kate's potential. Early in the novel, she meets a Mrs Norris, not a character to reappear, just an aside, but an interesting, working, single woman. 'From the first instant, Kate respected her for her isolation and her dauntlessness. The world is made up of a mass of people and a few individuals' (PS, p. 38). For Kate is going to learn to question her own assumptions, is going to put to test every belief she has ever held in life – by taking the journey to Mexico and having the criticism of a primitive people put over her western way of life – which is ultimately the only way for change and growth in one's maturity.

Kate is, however, a beautiful mixture of thoughts and feelings, displaying the confusions of a modern woman. She begins to experience the awful vacuum of living alone, and feels the need to have some man there again, as a stop-gap. Then, as soon as that idea is raised, she has to face the other side of herself which is that, as soon as she has a man there, something in her is disgusted by him, repulsed by him. 'She was naturally quite free-handed and she left people their liberty . . . She had a strong life-flow of her own, and a certain assertive *joie-de-vivre* . . . her mother, her father, her sisters, her first husband, even her children whom she loved, and Joachim, for whom she had felt such passionate love, even these, being near her, filled her with a certain disgust and repulsion after a little while' (PS, p. 264).

Kate's new adventure, however, is to be brought to face the western part of herself. Cipriano, with whom she becomes involved, having first befriended the little Mexican Don Ramon, tells her a thing or two about her freedom and independence. He explains that though she assumes she is free, she is slave to western, Anglo-Saxon and American ideas. The way she dresses, does her

hair, has money and even believes she should be free, is a con-
ditioned way of thinking from America. '. . . you are *not* free. You
are compelled all the time to be thinking USA thoughts – *compelled* I
must say. You have not as much choice as a slave . . . you must
think these USA thoughts, about being a woman and being free . . .
you are afraid of a man such as me, because you think I should not
treat you *à l'américaine*. You are quite right. I should not treat you as
an American woman must be treated' (PS, p. 218). Kate plays with
the idea. At first, she is seduced by Cipriano's talk and his affection
for her. But it is not easy, to throw over a lifetime's conditioning and
reflexes. The proud, free Kate boils back to the surface. Cipriano
gives her a new name, Malintzi:

> 'I am not! I am only Kate, and I am only a woman. I mistrust all
> that other stuff' . . . He went away, leaving her rocking in anger
> on her terrace, in love again with her old self, and hostile to the
> new thing. She was thinking of London and Paris and New York,
> and all the people there . . . 'Malintzi! I am Kate Forrester, really. I
> am neither Kate Leslie nor Kate Taylor. I am sick of these men
> putting names over me. I was born Kate Forrester, and I shall die
> Kate Forrester' (PS, p. 387).

The conflicts in Kate continue. Teresa, who becomes Don
Ramon's woman, draws out many of the paradoxical feelings in
Kate. She wants to make a new sort of relationship with a man, but
why should it be on the man's terms, as these Mexican women seem
to play it? Surely that is wrong, or is it? Teresa is quiet and close-
mouthed, with an air of independence and authority, but unstated.
Kate is at first frightened of her. Teresa also is frightened of the
well-travelled, assertive white-skinned western woman. Then Kate
gets annoyed at herself, and starts to despise Teresa.

> . . . What a curious will the little dark woman had! What a subtle
> female power inside her rather skinny body! She had the power to
> make him into a big, golden full glory of a man . . . Yes, surely it
> was the *slave* approach. Surely she wanted nothing but sex from
> him, like a prostitute' . . . Was it right? Kate asked herself. Wasn't
> it degrading for a woman? (PS, pp. 413–14).

Teresa says to Kate, later in the novel, that she is a soldier woman.
Kate would fight with herself if she were alone in the world – which

is quite an apt summing up of many western women.

By the end of the novel, Kate knows her conflict. She is alone as usual. She does not know how to relax with the Mexicans. She always has to turn back to her individuality. But she makes her compromise, when given the feeling she will stay with Cipriano. As she weeps, she can admit to herself that she is a fraud. It's not them who reject her, '*I know all the time it is I who won't altogether want them. I want myself to myself. But I can fool them so they shan't find out*' (PS, p. 461).

CONNIE CHATTERLEY

Connie is my favourite of all Lawrence's female characters. She manages to be a mixture of the virtues and attributes of all her predecessors – and, at the same time, to be more alive and real than any of them. Connie feels deeply about everything. It is hard not to feel along with her. Lawrence wrote three versions of the final *Lady Chatterley's Lover*, which ironically are all now in print. I have used mainly the second version, *John Thomas and Lady Jane* (where Connie's lover is Parkin, not Mellors), since somehow it seems fresher to my eye. But I have also used the regular *Lady Chatterley's Lover*, where necessary. It has been said before that Lawrence wanted to make clear his views on sex, to show how uninterested he was in promiscuity and how interested he was in people getting back to an understanding of what was natural, earthy and real about human life. He also wanted to explore further other themes already used. Connie is partly the modern young woman we have seen in Ursula and Alvina, wondering what to make of life; tempted by the freedom offered, but also needing something greater in her life. She wants love, and a committed relationship with a man. Connie takes Ursula's relationship with Birkin into actuality. She also manages some of the dark primitive instinct, for love and sex, that Alvina must have known with Cicio, but we never saw; and that Kate knew with Cipriano, which again we never saw. Take Connie, as a character, first.

Like Ursula, Gudrun, or even Alvina, as a young woman in the novel, she is trapped. Not, this time, as a teenager about to get out, but as a woman who has already made the mistake of a wrong marriage. She married Clifford Chatterley, who had money and prestige, and the title to Wragby Hall. He became crippled in the war – man's world war, as Lawrence tells us – and is crippled as a human being ever after. Connie knows what is wrong with her. She is dead too. 'And sometimes she would cry to herself: I want my heart to open! Oh, I want my heart to open! I don't want it shut up like this, like a coffin! Oh, if only God, or Satan, or a man or a woman or a child, or anybody, would help me to open my heart, because I can't do it myself' (JTLJ, p. 41). She is not looking for sex, nor for an affair.

In Connie, we must be seeing young Frieda, trapped in marriage to Ernest Weekly, having affairs with the Nottinghamshire lace manufacturer, with Otto Gross in Germany, and ultimately finding Lawrence. She was dead too, till Lawrence awakened her. In *Lady Chatterley's Lover*, in fact, the description of the two sisters, Connie and Hilda, is even more reminiscent of Frieda and her sister Else:

> Both Hilda and Constance had had their tentative love affairs by the time they were eighteen . . . Why couldn't a girl be queenly, and give the gift of herself? . . . being a girl, one's whole dignity and meaning in life consisted in the achievement of an absolute, a perfect, a pure and noble freedom. What else did a girl's life mean? . . . so the girls were 'free', and went back to Dresden, and their music, and the university and the young men . . . In the actual sex-thrill within the body, the sisters nearly succumbed to the strange male power. But quickly they recovered themselves, took the sex-thrill as a sensation, and remained free (LCL, pp. 7–9).

But the Connie who feels trapped knew there was something that she was looking for. Like Ursula before her, she wanted aestheticism and beauty, and variety in her life. She knew about the world of art, in fact so far she had found that human contact had not meant as much to her as had the rapture and fulfilment she got from Beethoven symphonies, or from books like *Les Liaisons Dangereuses*, from poetry, or from pictures, or the sight of Florence in the sunshine, or even from a course of philosophy lectures.

As for sex, what she had known of it – and she had had brief experience of other men, before Clifford . . . Even if she had children, she did not imagine they would *really* have mattered deeply to her: not to her own, individual life . . . And that was life! . . . Constance accepted it with a certain stoicism, which nevertheless left her exposed to devastating storms from within (JTLJ, pp. 54–5).

What is most important for Connie, when she first sees Parkin washing in the woods, is that she finds something that brings her back to life. She has found something wonderful, aesthetic, and powerful enough to believe in, to worship, to have meaning. I see nothing dreadful or demeaning in the fact that Connie is allowed to worship Parkin's body. On the contrary, to think of a man writing about a woman and giving her the sense of passion, and energy, sufficient to adore a man's body, is to me very beautiful. Connie expresses for all young women, *their* feelings about men and sex. It is not submission, or giving way to something they do not like; it is sheer pleasure and ultimate fulfilment.

> A great soothing came over her heart, along with the feeling of worship. The sudden sense of pure beauty, beauty that was active and alive, had put worship into her heart again . . . worship had come into her, because she had seen a pure loveliness, that was alive, and that had touched the quick in her (JTLJ, p. 51).

Connie doesn't give in immediately, by any means. In fact, most of the novel now charts her modern woman's problems and confusions with finding this worship, this kind of physical love. It is the power of sex that is demanding. Call it phallic sex, as does Lawrence – or just pure physicality, earthiness, giving way to sexual feelings – it is the same effect. Connie, who had yearned for something more than herself, now finds with fear that it is likely to take her over. She feels the invasion, and fears the loss of her individuality, as would any woman who had already achieved a certain sense of self. 'She was afraid of loving him. She was afraid of letting herself go. It seemed so like throwing away the oars and trusting to the stream: which was a sensation that, above all others, she dreaded. Yet she loved him . . . Ah, she adored him! And she longed to abandon herself to the luxury of adoring him' (JTLJ, p. 133). It is rather like Gudrun wanting to play with the fantasy of being the childlike, clinging woman. How does a woman cope with the two realities? As Connie knows, it is easy to embark on these adventures, but they carry you away, even beyond yourself.

> She was aware of a strange woman wakened up inside herself, a woman at once fierce and tender . . . She felt herself full of wild, undirected power, that she wanted to let loose.

But, as she thinks, she can make herself angry and upset:

She felt his domination over her, and against this, even against the very love inside herself, she revolted like one of the Bacchae, madly calling on Iarchos, the bright phallus that had no independent personality behind it, but was pure ecstatic servant to the woman (JTLJ, pp. 134, 136).

Connie continues with her struggle. Like Gudrun, and Ursula, she toys with the ideas of free love and freedom of woman's spirit. 'She recognised, emotionally, that the idea of eternal love, or life-long love even, and the idea of marriage, had a disastrous effect upon the will . . . Let there be permanency if it happens so. But let there be no convention of permanency, especially in emotional or passional relationships' (JTLJ, p. 154), she argued with herself, from the secure vantage point of still being Lady Chatterley, of course. She knows her passion for Parkin, he inflames her, she even wants his children, which is the first time she has felt that urge. But her heart remains free, she tells herself. 'Clifford, she was attached to him personally. The other man held her with passion. Nothing, and nobody held her altogether, and she did not want it' (JTLJ, p. 157).

That is why I love Connie. She fights for this free spirit in herself. It takes time, more love, passion and some talk from Parkin to make her understand what she is fighting. Partly, she is afraid. She has always been afraid of something in life. Now, the fear is of letting go to this sexual passion and seeing where it will lead her. It is, of course, dangerous, unpredictable, uncontrollable ground. Then, too, she realised that part of her had been playing with him, like Lettie with George all those years ago, in the woods, wanting his love, wanting to feel he would always be there for her when she felt like awakening the feelings, but not being prepared to commit herself. 'She wanted the selfish pleasure of the contact, but not the submission to the subtle interweaving of her life with his, in creative fate . . . If there *has* to be a break, break with circumstance rather than with destiny, even if you are left a cripple' (JTLJ, p. 300). We leave Connie optimistic, hopeful, still slightly afraid. But honest and courageous. What more is there in life, anyway?

In his short stories, you will find many similar Lawrence women, exercised to a shorter degree, perhaps exploring one or two of the themes. None of them touches to the same degree the truths that the characters from the major novels reach, but they are worth noticing. There is Mary in 'The Daughers of the Vicar'; Juliet in 'The Sun'; 'The

Woman Who Rode Away'; Lou in 'St Mawr'; the sisters again in 'The Virgin and the Gipsy'; and March in 'The Fox'. All recognisable, all speaking to us as modern women with the conflicts and paradoxes of the contemporary age, that Lawrence understood so well in woman.

4 Duality

Lawrence, as we have already seen, was set on a new endeavour for his age – to become a 'man-and-woman' in his life, and particularly in the expression of his ideas through the novels. He was exploring with great boldness the female mode of being. As a dominating intellectual concept, he also devoted his critical essays, and monologues, to a large extent, to an elaboration of the theme, for Lawrence based all his theories on the complicated concept of duality. There is a tension set up throughout every aspect of life created by the opposites from which life is formed. This tension is at once the most constructive and destructive force – it is exciting and terrifying. The concept of duality fits well with eastern modes of thinking that became more popular in the later twentieth century after Lawrence's death. One can imagine he might have fitted well with the sixties growth of travel and seeking of new cultures that took so many young people out to the east. But, unfortunately for Lawrence, it was still a conservative world he lived in and, as ever, he was the outsider.

Duality is quite easy to come to terms with: it is the theory that opposites do more than attract, they are firmly held together in eternal combustion; they repel, attract and at base are firmly linked. Lawrence saw the duality in everything: in being a human being, 'For every man comprises male and female in his being . . . A woman likewise consists of male and female' (STH, p. 93). His *Study of Thomas Hardy* explores the ideas, as theory, most fully and most comprehensibly. They turn up in even later works such as the 'Fantasia of the Unconscious', but often his writing is too bitty and rambling by that stage. I would advise anyone to read the Thomas Hardy work, however, as an insight into the ideas behind Lawrence's novels.

Sex, says Lawrence, 'is only a definite indication of the great male and female duality and unity . . . There is female apart from

Woman, as we know, and male apart from Man . . . part of the great twin river each branch resistant to the other, eternally running each to meet the other . . . until eternity there shall be this separateness, this interaction of man upon woman, imperfection . . . Every impulse that stirs in life, every single impulse, is either male or female, distinct . . . This is the complete movement; upon woman, woman within man. This is the desire, the achieving of which, frictionless, is impossible . . .' (STH, p. 55). He repeats the variations on the theme over and over, until you have to understand. It is the very root of Lawrentian theory of the force that constantly pulls men and women together and forces them apart. This section is my own favourite:

> . . . it is as if life were a double cycle, of man and woman, facing opposite ways, travelling opposite ways, revolving upon each other . . . reaching forward with outstretched hand, and neither able to move till their hands have grasped each other . . . each travelling in his separate cycle (STH, p. 61).

Those words could combine as the refrain for all Lawrence's writings on what he himself described as the relationships between man and woman that are so important in these days. Readers today can learn more about the conflicts and paradoxes in the man/woman relationship by reading Lawrence than they can from hours of expensive therapy.

Where Lawrence himself learned these theories is unknown. Edward Carpenter has said that Rousseau is often used as Lawrence's precursor, as he too treated in similar vein the deep-seated conflict between natural and cosmic man; man in touch with the instinctive, with the pristine nakedness of nature and the artificial state of civilisation. Then, too, as Martin Green has explained, Lawrence was much influenced by the Schwabing Circle in Munich whose ideas percolated through to him from Frieda. One writer from that circle was Ludwig Klages, whose work *The Mind the Soul's Enemy* contains the major proportion of what has become Lawrence's own branch of metaphysics. Klages states that the soul and the body are two poles of natural life in man. Mind, which works by abstraction and logic, fixes the movement of that polarity, creating an artificial world of concepts, hostile to natural life. It distorts experience. This is an idea which Lawrence often puts over in the novels. Klages's *'blutleuchte'* has a lot in common with

Lawrence's 'blood-knowledge', or intuition, which he too used to mean non-rational knowledge.

Lawrence did not explain his theories only in *The Study of Thomas Hardy*. Other later essays, such as 'The Crown' and 'The Two Principles', are also devoted to duality. 'The Crown' was first published in 1915, but reappeared in *Reflections on the Death of a Porcupine*, in 1925. This is an important volume of essays, many of which, however, are extremely dull, as Lawrence goes off on tangents and sermons. In 'The Crown' he goes further into the theme of duality. They are two seas which eternally attract and oppose each other, . . . which foam upon one another, as the ocean foams on the land, and the land rushes down into the sea' (P, p. 372). Then there is his theory on the great clash that causes birth: 'the clash of the two into one', or 'the foam being thrown up into consummation'. Or, in 'The Two Principles', originally written as part of his series of essays on American Literature, Lawrence writes on cosmic duality:

> In procreation, the two germs of the male and female epitomize the two cosmic principles, as these are held within the life spell . . . Life can never be produced or made. Life is an unbroken oneness, indivisible . . .

> We have first the mystic dualism of pure otherness, that which science will not admit, . . . This dualism extends through everything, even through the *soul* or *self* or *being* of any living creature . . . *within* the self, which is single, the principle of dualism reigns (P, pp. 230–3).

These writings show Lawrence's knowledge of some eastern writing and ideas. He describes the mystic dualism as part of the three Chinese sacred mysteries – the sex division, which is pure otherness, pure dualism, like the opposites fire and water.

> Through the gates of the eyes and nose and mouth and ears, through the delicate ports of the fingers, through the great window of the yearning breast, we pass into our oneness with the universe, our great extension of being, towards infinitude. But in the lower part of the body there is darkness and pivotal pride . . . (P, p. 235).

He also quotes what he describes as 'the ancients', who called the heart the seat of understanding. He agrees with them: that there we find primal understanding, 'the seat of passional self-consciousness'. To Lawrence, that blind direction created by sex, the force of one being to the other, is far more important than any rationalised love, for it is the instinct, the intuition, the 'blood knowledge'. All the strength of the natural world forces combustion, disintegration, merging, and manages to break down any carefully constructed walls based on sound sense and judgement.

Taking the concept of duality further, he constructs theories of duality based on the body as symbol of the consciousness. There is the opposition between the breast and the bowels. The breast denotes something ethereal, and refined, which seeks upwards and outwards to the universe, and things spiritual. The bowels, however, are seen as the 'dark whirlwind of pristine force . . . not concerned to look out, or to consider itself beyond' (P, p. 236). There we have encapsulated the opposition between the spiritual force yearning outward, beyond, to something more ideal, and the physical force interested only in seething darkness, dragging us back. Or, again, he defines it as the duality between face and loins. In the face we see, perceive, and, in delight, become part of all things in the universe. In the loins, we have roots, 'There deep calls unto deep. There in the sexual passion the very blood surges into communion, in the terrible sensual oneing'.

The ideas may seem complicated stated as stark theory, but once dramatised by Lawrence in the novels they leap off the page. His basic concept of the tension of opposites runs through every work. The concept is one of the polarity, the negative and positive, there in all human relationships – which you can tie up with Jungian theory of integration if you prefer a more contemporary interpretation. The man/woman relationship is seen by Lawrence as a double reconciliation of opposites (Dal, pp. 13–15). For man and woman not only have to meet as opposites, but also to reconcile the opposing forces within themselves. Dividing them into men and women is arbitrary, which is where Lawrence was really one step beyond his latter-day feminist critics. His total concept is much deeper than they suppose. Daleski, in *The Forked Flame*, says that to see the male and female as different is as arbitrary as seeing motion and rest as totally separate. They are the same when seen completely. For Lawrence, it is 'centrifugal for the male, fleeing abroad, away from the centre, outward to infinite vibration, and centripetal for the female, fleeing in to the eternal centre of the rest'. The balance between the male and female, found in individual men or women, divides like the eastern concept of the yin and the yang, provides differences and balancing properties: such as movement/stability, activity/ permanence, the one who registers relationships/the one occupied with self-feeling; the one refusing sensation/the one submitting to sensation; multiplicity/oneness; knowledge/feeling; love/law; spirit/flesh; abstraction/fulfilment through the senses; knowledge/ nature; brain/body; light/dark and discovery/to belief in origins (Dal, p. 30). Following those opposites, we can see where the Lawrentian lead of the female mode of being was taking him.

The man/woman tension of opposites in the novels is dramatic and colourful. Lawrence builds up his female characters into Woman, for to him that is how men see women – as the individual but also as symbol of all Women. Lydia Lensky, when having her baby, looks at old Tom, 'as a woman in childbirth looks at the man who begot the child in her; an impersonal look, in the extreme hour, female to male . . . There was the infinite world, eternal, un- changing, as well as the world of life' (R, p. 81). Or, when Tom and Anna are considering their battle with each other, Toms reflects, 'He could leave her only for another woman . . . Besides, he would be just in the same state. Another woman would be woman, the case would be the same . . . The only other way to leave her was to die . . . But he had no desire for death' (R, p. 187).

Ursula, like Anna, explores the essence of femaleness in her relationships with her men. Ursula, capable of being even more cruel than Anna, more or less uses Skrebensky as a testing ground for her female powers, to see just how far she can go. 'She could limit and define herself against him, the male, she could be her maximum self, female, oh female, triumphant for one moment in exquisite assertion against the male, in supreme contradistinction to the male' (R, p. 303). Later, in *Women in Love*, we find Birkin who, as the Lawrence figure, most actively contemplates the theme of duality, reflecting on Ursula as woman; 'She was rich, full of dangerous power. She was like a strange unconscious bud of powerful womanhood. He was unconsciously drawn to her. She was his future'. Birkin is allowed to express the Lawrentian theory in its full abstraction. Ursula asks him, 'Still a man has very little need for a woman now, has he?' and Birkin's reply is familiar to those who have previously read the Lawrence essays:

In outer things, maybe – except to share his bed and bear his children. But essentially, there is just the same need as there ever was. Only nobody takes the trouble to be essential . . . I do think . . . that the world is only held together by the mystic conjunction, the ultimate unison between people – a bond. And the immediate bond is between man and woman (R, p. 169).

Further, Birkin theorises:

We are not broken fragments of one whole . . . The man is pure man, the woman pure woman, they are perfectly polarised . . . There is only the pure duality of polarisation, each one free from any contamination of the other . . . Each has a single, separate being, with its own laws. The man has his pure freedom, the woman hers . . . Each admits the different nature in the other (WL, p. 225).

For Gerald, in his relationship with Gudrun, Lawrence brings out the element of mother worship in the man's attitude towards woman: '. . . she was the great bath of life, he worshipped her. Mother and substance of all life she was. And he, child and man, received of her and was made whole' (WL, p. 389). To round it all off, there is Birkin at his most elevated, bringing the two opposing poles together into the great mystic oneness. This is the essence of Birkin's theories on relationships. Man and woman are single and individual, and should be able to come together, in that form, in a relationship; through which separateness they achieve the perfect oneness, unity and wholeness, not of merging and submission, but of maintaining the separateness:

. . . there was no I and you, there was only the third, unrealised wonder, the wonder of existing not as oneself, but in a consummation of my being and of her being in a new one, a new paradisal unit regained from the duality . . . we are both caught up and transcended into a new oneness where everything is silent, . . . all is perfect and at one . . . in the perfect One there is perfect silence of bliss (WL, p. 417).

So Birkin and Ursula make it? One doubts it.

Strangely enough, it is in the novel *Kangaroo*, written some years later, that the character of that name, a rather boorish very overtly male person of Lawrence's later life, most succinctly states the theory of togetherness and separateness: 'I believe the sun's attraction for the earth is a form of love.' Somers, who in *Kangaroo* is the Lawrence figure, asks, 'Then why doesn't the earth fly into the sun?' And Kangaroo's reply is of the attraction and repulsion that is similar to love between man and woman.

> The earth and the sun, on their plane, have discovered a perfect equilibrium. But man has not yet begun . . . so far, but rarely, rarely has he *consciously* known that he could only love her for her own separate, strange self: forever strange, and a joyful mystery to him . . . The tangible unknown (K, p. 149).

Kate Leslie, also as an expression of the later Lawrence feeling more disillusioned about man's achievement of perfection, in *The Plumed Serpent*, puts a more jaded view of this separateness:

> She had thought that each individual had a complete self, a complete soul, an accomplished I . . . Men and women had incomplete selves, made up of bits assembled together loosely and somewhat haphazard . . . A world full of half-made creatures on two legs, eating food and degrading the one mystery left to them, sex (PS, p. 115).

Or, as the author says further in the novel, 'Though a woman be dearer to a man than his own life, yet he is still he, and she is she, and the gulf can never close up'.

However, the theory of duality is in reality easier to live with than the substance. The very concept of duality comes from the noun 'dual' – and in that we have a clue. From the duality comes the battle we all know so well, particularly in the man/woman relationship. As Lawrence has put it elsewhere, there is the eternal force of attraction and repulsion, 'I resist, yet am compelled'. In his own life, we know that Lawrence suffered from this tension of opposites. In his early dealings with women, for example with Jessie Chambers, he suffered the feeling of being absorbed, taken over, by a woman who wanted his soul. In a letter to Rachel Annand Taylor, about Louie Burrows, he wrote,

> Nobody can have the soul of me. My mother had had it, and nobody can have it again. Nobody can come into my very self again, and breathe me like an atmosphere . . . Louie, whom I

wish to marry the day after the funeral – she would never demand to drink me up and have me. She loves me – but it is a fine, warm, healthy natural love, not the Jane Eyre who is Muriel (Jessie), but like say Rhoda Fleming of Anna Karenina. She will never plunge her hands through my blood and feel for my soul, and make me set my teeth and shiver and fight away. Ugh . . .

When he met Frieda, however, he changed his mind again, wanting a relationship with a woman who would make him think and fight. The *Look We Have Come Through* volume of poems reflects their honeymoon and is nakedly confessional about their happiness and misery: just the titles show the kinds of drama being acted out – 'And oh, that the man I am might cease to be', 'Mutilation', 'Song of a man who is not loved', 'Why does she weep?', 'Loggerheads', compared to, 'Roses on the breakfast table', 'Paradise re-entered', 'Song of man who has come through', and 'Elysium'. After this episode, he wrote in a letter to Mrs Sallie Hopkin, 'Frieda and I have struggled through some bad times into a wonderful naked intimacy, all kindled with warmth, that I know at last is love. I think I ought not to blame women, as I have done, but myself, for taking my love to the wrong woman, before now . . . at any rate I do love, and I am loved. I have given and I have taken – and that is eternal' (L, 19 August 1912).

In 'The Two Principles', he again talks about the kind of battles that happen between men and women locked in the polarity: 'The coming-together of the sexes may be the soft, delicate union of pure creation, or it may be the tremendous conjunction of opposition, a vivid struggle, as fire struggles with water in the sun' (P, p. 234). It is the struggle that we see most clearly in the novels. This is the theme of his men and women: the battle of the sexes, the eternal will to belong, and fear of being submerged. Lawrence, in another late essay, 'Love Was Once a Little Boy', described most eloquently the essence of loving:

. . . love, as a desire, is balanced against the opposite desire, to maintain the integrity of the individual self. Hate is not the opposite of love. The real opposite of love is individuality. We live in the age of individuality, we call ourselves servants of love. That is to say, we enact a perpetual paradox (P, p. 444).

Thus we have Lawrence the realist, beneath the level of the theorist, who knew what contemporary relationships are like because he was living one. Talking about the love between a man and a woman, he says, 'As sure as you start with a case of "true love" between them, you end with a terrific struggle and conflict of the two opposing egos and individualities . . . Love as a relationship of unison, means and must mean, to some extent, the sinking of the individuality'. He calls it by a nice phrase, 'the scrimmage of love'. If there is no flame, there is not the same conflict or fight . . . But that is no ideal state either. Too many modern marriages, he finds, as he says in the essay 'A Propos of *Lady Chatterley's Lover*', are based on a pairing of people for similarities rather than opposites, which is friendship between the sexes, not love. To Lawrence, this is not real marriage and, though realistic, he can say quite straightforwardly, 'In people of strong, individual feeling the irritation that accumulates in marriage increases only too often to a point of rage that is akin to madness' (P, p. 507). This is what all the Lawrence novels claim, more than anything; the 'perpetual paradox' and the 'rage akin to madness'. It is what I call the love-sex-conflict theme of Lawrence's work.

Anna and Will Brangwen are the first couple really to show the Lawrentian force of battle, in *The Rainbow*:

> So it went on continually, the recurrence of love and conflict between them . . . One day she thought she would go mad from his very presence . . . The next day she loved and rejoiced in the way he crossed the floor, he was sun, moon and stars in one . . . She was uneasy. The surety, the surety, the inner surety, the confidence in the abidingness of love: that was what she wanted. And that she did not get . . . They fought an unknown battle, unconsciously. Still they were in love with each other, the passion was there. But the passion was consumed in a battle (R, pp. 167–8).

The relationship develops, increasing not in harmony but in the passion and intensity of their feelings, polarised. After the birth of baby Ursula, Will becomes like a madman:

> It was a duel: no love, no words, no kisses even, only the maddening perception of beauty consummate, absolute through touch . . . He was obsessed . . . He wished he had a hundred men's energies, with which to enjoy her . . . He wanted to wallow in her, bury himself in her flesh, cover himself over with her flesh (R, p. 236).

Ursula, very much the daughter of Anna, carries forward her mother's powerful intensity into her relationship as a young woman with Skrebensky. Here the two of them are eloquently described locked in one variation of the eternal battle. Ursula is the powerful one, and Skrebensky, appalled at her power, yet loves it and lets himself be taken over. Ursula, in *Women in Love*, does not continue with such actions. She meets Birkin and meets her match. She and Birkin do not fight, in the novel as written by Lawrence, because through the two of them Lawrence is trying to draw an idealised picture of the perfect relationship. But any reader can imagine what might have happened after the last page of the novel. Here though, in *The Rainbow*, is the young Ursula in full battle:

. . . a sudden lust seized her, to lay hold of him and tear him and make him into nothing. Her hands and wrists felt immeasurably hard and strong, like blades . . . He strove subtly, but with all his energy, to enclose her, to have her . . . She took him in the kiss, hard her kiss seized upon him . . . She seemed to be destroying him . . . And her soul crystallised with triumph, and his soul was dissolved with agony and annihilation . . . She had triumphed: he was not any more (R, pp. 321–2).

It is in *Aaron's Rod*, not one of Lawrence's better-known, or even better novels, that we get a glimpse of yet another most vivid and colourful husband/wife battle, from the duality of their relationship. This involves Aaron, who has walked out on his wife Lottie and child. Remembering their married life together, we get this portrait: 'She could never understand whence arose in her, almost from the first days of marriage with him, her terrible paroxysms of hatred for him. She was in love with him; ah heaven, how maddeningly she was in love with him . . . But in revulsion, how she hated him!' (AR, p. 193). It is in Parkin (or Mellors) and Connie in the novel *John Thomas and Lady Jane*, that we meet most of the duality and fight that comes from the sex instinct in men and women. Parkin is described as a man who was born solitary and yet he had the true sex desire more strongly than most men. Because it had been humiliated by his wife, he preferred to keep himself alone. It is Parkin who stirs up in Connie the true sex desire; and the very essential sexuality of that novel comes from the sense of their separateness coming together. It is that excitement that manages to pass across to the reader, and hence it becomes the most erotic of his novels. Connie particularly expresses the 'perpetual paradox'; the terrible desire to give way to this man, and the equally terrible fear of doing so, and the will to hold herself back.

From the beginning of their relations, Parkin curses himself that he let himself get involved. It is too dangerous, he knows that: '. . . by taking the woman, by going forth naked to her, he had exposed himself to he knew not what fear, and doom' (JTLJ, p. 122). While Connie goes through even worse conflicts: '. . . she felt his domination over her, and against this, even against the very love inside herself, she revolted like one of the Bacchae . . . The man, the mere man, with his independent soul and personality, let him not dare to intrude' (JTLJ, pp. 135–6). It is at the end of *John Thomas and Lady Jane* that Connie realises she can give in, and by doing so, in all awareness, not lose but gain.

The other theme that comes out of this battle between two polar-ised sexes is the threat of the will to dominate one or the other, and the struggle of the individual's ego to do so. Lawrence's view was that it is individuality that is the opposite of love, not hate. It is will that destroys the balance, and which Lawrence pinpoints as being a culpable manifestation of 'head' action, not 'bowel' action. Anna and Will Brangwen again experience the primal pain of this conflict. 'Anna, . . . realised that she was being borne down by him, borne down by the clinging, heavy weight of him . . . her life, her freedom, was sinking under the silent grip of his physical will. He wanted her in his power. He wanted to devour her at leisure, to have her . . . Then she turned fiercely on him, and fought him' (R, p. 185). In Anna, and years later when he was drawing the character of Connie, for *John Thomas and Lady Jane*, Lawrence gave women the ultimate expression of their fear of dominance from men; which is why it is hard to understand how feminists can attack Lawrence for not sympathising with women. Any woman can see herself in these conflicts going on in Connie, or Anna. 'Tonight she realised' – this is Connie learning to accept what is happening; learning that sub-mission to Parkin is not defeat to a man, but accepting the fear and ecstasy of a passionate love – 'The root of the fear had been fear of the phallus. This is the root-fear of all mankind . . . There was something that danger could not touch: one thing and one body: the perfect sleeping circle of the male and female, phallic body' (JTLJ, p. 239).

In *The Plumed Serpent*, Lawrence places even more emphasis on the will as the destructive force in natural uninhibited relationships.

Here it is not just men imposing their will on women, but the opposite battle of women trying to impose their individual egos over men. Kate Leslie, because she is a western woman, tempted by the ideas of a more primitive people, faces the 'perpetual paradox' in a new and enlightening way. At once she is fascinated to find herself totally under Cipriano's will, and finds the new passivity in herself interesting. Then, 'she could not be purely this, this thing of sheer reciprocity', and instinct tells her to fight against it. Lawrence definitely maintains that these Mexican people with their strong roots in the primeval, in the instinct, were stronger than she. They might appear to acquiesce to her will, because she looked strong, as a western woman, accustomed to ruling. But really they were demanding more of her. The assertion was what he describes as 'of the blood' – that is of instinct, of powerful natural forces. 'It was the assertion that swept away all individualism, and left her immersed, drowned in the grand sea of living blood.'

The battle, also a strong part of the Lawrentian theme of duality between naturalism and civilising influences, is often most clearly seen in the women in the novels. Many critics have devoted themselves to the explanation of this part of the Lawrence theme. Nature stands for the natural self, the body, and silence. Culture stands for the social self, mind, language. It is the other form of essential opposites, from which tension the novels derive life. Kate Leslie, in *The Plumed Serpent*, is to me the best symbol of this kind of conflict, as she reflects on the ambivalence in herself of a divided nature, between naturalism and culture, 'she was aware of the duality in herself', he says at one point, and the novel is in effect the story of her struggle for reintegration.

Kate reflects on the sight of the Indians in the University: how all the progress, socialism and culture in the world would not help the primitive tribesman. The Indians 'were figures of the pathos of the victims of modern industry and capitalism' (PS, p. 58). She reflects often on the Mexican women, with their long skirts, dark looks, and primeval sensuality, 'they were images of wild submissiveness, the primitive womanliness of the world, . . . the dark eyes of half-created women, soft, appealing, yet with a queer void insolence' (PS, p. 84). To Kate, a modern woman, there is something almost insulting in their passivity, their seemingly submissive stance to their men. She wants to understand more deeply what femaleness is; whether these women are actually more womanly than she, in her modern brittle way, can ever be. Whether it is Kate who is wrong, or them. It is not all a question of men and women, for Kate. She knows what she yearns for – which is for some of the magic to be put back in life, 'to let the sunwise world steal across to her, and add its motion to her, the motion of the stress of life, with the big sun and the stars like a tree holding out its leaves'. So, she cries aloud to the 'great mystery' and asks the 'life-breath' to come into her.

Anna Brangwen, of *The Rainbow*, feels the split between the primeval and her modern self no less. After giving of herself to her instincts, for the few days after her marriage, she gets up from the bed, and appeals to the outside world once more. She wanted the dead world back, and to that end she gave a tea party to her women friends. Even Lawrence seems to accept that no one can live in his dark, primitive world every day. While, for Will Brangwen, it is the birth of Ursula that makes him want to sweep away the 'whole monstrous superstructure of the world of today, cities and industries and civilisation, leave only the bare earth with plants growing and waters running, and he would not mind . . .' (R, p. 193). Whereas the much-reviled Hermione, of *Women in Love*, is drawn as a woman who has brought mind only in to play. Even her interest in passion and animal instincts has been consciously aroused as a 'head' effort, says Birkin accusingly. 'Because you haven't got any real body, any dark sensual body of life. You have no sensuality' (WL, p. 46). Birkin is quite as keen as Kate Leslie in getting to know the savage, the primitive. He stands gazing at a statue of a savage woman, and reflects how she is 'Pure culture in sensation, culture in the physical consciousness, really ultimate physical consciousness, mindless, utterly sensual'. And again, for Birkin, it is the statuette of an African goddess that unleashes his train of thought. To him the West Africans know more about the phallic knowledge he so much wanted to become a part of. 'The white races, having the Arctic north behind them, the vast abstraction of ice and snow would fulfil a mystery of ice destructive knowledge, snow abstract annihilation' (WL, p. 286), and in those words we can surely hear the echo of Lawrence the author.

In his last great work, leading up to the final publication of *Lady Chatterley's Lover*, Lawrence puts similar ideas more fully, in the version that is *John Thomas and Lady Jane*. The novel was written just after Lawrence's last, miserable return to his native land, when he looked with horror on the industrial ravages of his Nottinghamshire homeland, and on the sad white faces of the people whose spirit had been crushed. This time, his feelings express not so much the duality, or conflict within his characters, but his own sheer antipathy to this industrialised world. It explains why he had grown more at home in Italy, or Mexico, or any country with a more primitive culture.

[Connie] realised there were two main sorts of energy, the frictional, seething, resistant, explosive, blind sort, like that of steam engines and motor cars and electricity, such people as Clifford and Bill Tewson and modern, insistent women, and these queer vacuous miners: then there was the other, forest energy, that was still and softly powerful, with tender, frail bud-tips and gentle finger-ends full of awareness. She herself was seized by both kinds of energy . . . And Parkin stood to her for this peace (JTLJ, p. 371).

5 Relationships

At the centre of all Lawrence's work is his view on the relationship between man and woman: the modern definition of the time-honoured liaison or battle between the sexes. A true perception of what Lawrence was offering in his definition of the word 'relationship' is vital for an understanding of his attitude towards both women and men. When Lawrence talks of 'relationship', he talks in terms of a committed, one-to-one, intense, creative partnership akin to the marriage relationship. He does not, contrary to popular opinion in his time and still to some extent now, mean promiscuous sex, or free love, or any of the more fashionable ideas. Lawrence means what today we have come to call the 'creative relationship'; one in which man and woman come to meet as opposites, as equals, as similar but different, as potential partners, and enemies in a duel; who through their feelings for each other test themselves, learn about each other and go beyond the normal social confines of either 'marriage' or casual sex that Lawrence so hated. He saw both extremes as a waste of life, a waste of the essential life-force, of the potential that is in each human being.

Lawrence stated that he would do his life's work sticking up for the relationship between man and woman. He has defined the new type of woman, through Ursula and Gudrun, the 'self-responsible' woman looking for her own career, her independence and freedom from social restrictions, a life not constrained by parents, environment or husband's values. Gudrun: 'One must be free, above all, one must be free . . . No man will be sufficient to make that good, no man!' Ursula, too, is given those headstrong qualities while at the same time knowing there is a 'big want' deep in her. The want is for some form of love with a man, with a human being, that will make sense of her life.

Lawrence has also clarified how he sees man and woman as two individuals, struggling to work out how they can live side by side. In this he was original, the begetter of the later twentieth-century system of values that still causes pain and conflict in the people trying to live them out – for woman has to be seen as an independent being as the first step. But the man who wrote, 'It is as if life were a double cycle, of man and woman, facing opposite ways, travelling opposite ways, revolving upon each other . . . reaching forward with outstretched hand, and neither able to move till their hands have grasped each other . . . each travelling in his separate cycle', was not trying to establish a pattern that can loosely be described as male chauvinist, that of dominant man seeking submission of woman. He was trying to find something different.

Lawrence was not writing about the man–woman relationship in limbo, nor just theorising. Like most novelists, he had his own experience to bring to bear. And, interestingly, what might have been pure theory from the young Lawrence soon mellowed and evolved, not away from the idealism, but further into it, evolving from his relationship with Frieda. From his letters we get signals of what was going on between them. The letters change in their tone within days, from the ecstatic, as a young man who finds all his hopes of passion fulfilled: 'I love Frieda so much, I don't like to talk about it. I never knew what love was before . . . The world is wonderful and beautiful and good beyond one's wildest imagination. Never, never, never could one conceive what love is, beforehand, never. Life *can* be great – quite godlike. It *can* be so . . . Love is a much bigger thing than passion, and a woman *much* more than sex' (L, 2 June 1912). Taking the deliberations and frustrations of Paul Morel, in *Sons and Lovers,* to be an indication of the processes suffered by Lawrence himself searching for love, sex and the right woman, it is an indication that in fact, when he found her, he got more than his imagination could ever have conjured up. Which is why we have to believe that many great novelists write from direct experience, not from the so-often revered imagination. Truth is more significant, and more people relate to it. The other side of their relationship was described a few weeks later by Lawrence, 'we are in no danger of being killed with kindness or surfeited with sweet'. Or later, as he puts it, 'We've had some hard times, Frieda and I. It is not so easy for a man and a woman to live alone together in a foreign country for six months, and dig out a love deeper and deeper'. It is in that letter that he ends by saying he will do his work for women, 'better than the Suffrage' (L, 23 December 1912).

The lessons he learned, and to which he devoted so many novels, were that love is not easy, it is ever-changing, and not how oneself had imagined it. 'One must learn to love, and go through a good deal of suffering to get to it, like any knight of the grail, and the journey is always *towards* the other soul, not away from it, . . . To love, you have to learn to understand the other, more than she understands herself, and to submit to her understanding of you . . . Your most vital necessity in this life is that you shall love your wife completely and implicitly and in entire nakedness of body and spirit' (L, 7 July 1914).

It was through meeting Frieda that he started to rewrite his great work *The Sisters,* and the final version of *The Rainbow* was much influenced by his knowledge of this type of woman and type of relationship. He wrote a letter about *The Sisters,* 'I can only write what I feel pretty strongly about: and that, at present, is the relation between men and women. After all, it is *the* problem of today, the establishment of a new relation, or the readjustment of the old one, between men and women' (L, 17 March 1914). It is ironic, thinking of Lawrence's short lifetime, that we are only now really entering that phase. That after a fuller version of the women's movement, freer education, more jobs for women, relaxation of social mores over marriage and children, we have finally allowed the individual man and woman to work out the relationship that best suits them. It is already fifty years since Lawrence, the prophet, died. We should feel proud to have inherited his vision.

What Lawrence saw as the suburban marriage was the real danger, 'more a duel than a duet' he described it, and 'fatal boredom'. More than mere legal marriage, he strove for 'absolute mystic marriage'. He was asking a lot of one man and one woman, banking their hopes and idealism on each other – but through Lawrence we can feel the energy of a society in change and transition; the same English provincial, industrialised society that he had grown to hate so much. Martin Green compares Lawrence's thinking to that of Frieda's ex-lover and tutor in life, Otto Gross. Gross, says Martin Green (MG, p. 70), had a vision of a society ruined by repressed sexual energy: this led to hysterical women who expend masses of energy either in repressing their sexuality or in giving it an unnatural, but socially acceptable form, in the institution of marriage. In men, the equivalent repressed sexual instinct comes out either in aggressive action or in its opposite, pathological cowardice. Gross maintained that the state is basically homosexual 'its hierarchical authority lays men prone one beneath another'. Gross followed the theory through, linking it with the Cosmic Circle's ideas on eroticism:

> to love erotically is not to feel identified with the other person, but with the third being, the relationship itself. Erotic love alone can finally overcome man's loneliness. Relationship understood is that third thing, that worshipped as a supreme value, will allow the lover to combine an erotic union with an uncompromised drive to individuality.

We can feel Lawrence in most of that statement: the combination of erotic union, with the belief in the third force which is the love between two people, and the drive, without compromise, towards one's own individuality.

For the expression of these ideas in the novels, we need look no further than Birkin, in *Women in Love*. Birken is the most Lawrentian of men, in that he is Lawrence's direct mouthpiece. He is little else, however, as there is no real character or substance to Birkin. What he does for a living, how he grew up, what he feels when Ursula responds to him, are not given much space; all we hear are Birkin's theories on the dual relationship. As such, they are extremely interesting. To Birkin is given all the talk of the great explorer on the marriage theme: 'It is death to oneself – but it is the coming into being of another', is the gist of his feelings. The individual is there, intact, but the former individual dies as the two become one and two separate beings. In the earlier section of the novel, Birkin talks these ideas over with Gerald, and so we got the male point of view:

> [Birkin] 'I find', he said, 'that one needs some one *really* pure single activity – I should call love a single pure activity. But I *don't* really love anybody – not now.' [That was before Ursula.] [Gerald] 'I don't believe a woman, and nothing but a woman, will ever make my life.'

> [Birkin] 'The old ideals are dead as nails – nothing there. It seems to me there remains only this perfect union with a woman – a sort of ultimate marriage – and there isn't anything else' (WL, pp. 63–4).

When Birkin meets Ursula, he sees in her the potential for this ultimate marriage, and to her surprise, rather than courting her with the old-fashioned words of romance, sentiment and love, he flings his soul down before her and tries to tempt her to his new world, his exacting, demanding, searching prospect of marriage. Ursula is not impressed, at first. She responds as one might to his high-flown theories: 'You mean you don't love me?' Birkin – 'The root is beyond love . . . there beyond, where there is no speech and no terms of agreement.' He calls it, 'not meeting and mingling', but a 'strange conjunction' and, his theme tune, 'an equilibrium, a pure balance of two single beings: – as the stars balance each other' (WL, pp. 161–4).

Ursula believes he is proposing old-fashioned marriage, but that he is scared of real commitment. She tries to tell him that if he loved her, he would be talking of loving no one but her – 'If you admit a unison, you forfeit all the possibilities of chaos'. She is saying that when lovers commit themselves to each other, they tie themselves to each other, they shut off all the outside doors. Chaos and freedom are not compatible concepts. Birkin argues back that her words, such as 'love is freedom', are mere 'sentimental cant' which she has picked up from others, and she is merely mouthing them. He tries to go over with her why love *is* selfish, or can afford to be – why it is not a question of irresolutely tying yourself to one other person. 'It is not selfless – it is a maintaining of the self in mystic balance, and integrity – like a star balanced with another star' (WL, p. 170).

Birkin voices Lawrence's fears of the old-fashioned views of love and marriage, 'the old way of love seems a dreadful bondage', and says 'He would rather not live than accept the love she proffered'. To him, 'The hot narrow intimacy between man and wife was abhorrent. The way they shut their doors these married people, and shut themselves into their own exclusive alliance with each other, even in love, disgusted him . . . a kaleidoscope of couples, disjoined, separatist, meaningless entities of married couples . . .' (WL, p. 223). Birkin again explains how he wants to be single in himself, and the woman single in herself, but both always held together by the force of the duality, the tension between, the sheer beauty of the mystic balance, that means they could not part. Referring back to one of Lawrence's letters, we can see he felt that himself, in his own life. After weeks of battles with Frieda, the highs and the lows, he was able to write – 'Once you've known what love can be, there's no disappointment any more, and no despair. If the skies tumble down like a smashed saucer, it couldn't break what's between Frieda and me. I think folk have got sceptic about love – that's because nearly everybody fails' (L, 25 December 1912).

So Birkin is able to disparage Ursula for her old-fashioned
thinking, which from the picture already drawn of Ursula we know
she does not really feel. But here the fearful side of her does not
know what to make of Birkin's bizarre proposition. He sees the old
clinging woman rearing her ugly head through Ursula's modern
make-up, which was very likely.

> . . .[woman] had such a lust for possession, a greed of self-
> importance in love. She wanted to have, to own, to control, to be
> dominant. Everything must be referred back to her, to Woman, the
> Great Mother of everything, out of whom proceeded everything
> and to whom everything must finally be rendered up . . . Man was
> hers because she had borne him. A Mater Dolorosa, she had borne
> him, a Magna Mater, she now claimed him again, soul and body,
> sex, meaning, and all . . . We are not broken fragments of one
> whole (WL, pp. 224–5).

But Ursula had a right to question his high-sounding theories, for
what did Birkin really want? Was he not really just excusing himself
for that male fear of commitment to woman? Was he not arguing he
could have her and his freedom? Was he not laying down the terms,
to get them in before she did, so that he would dominate her life and
she would have to submit in accepting his terms? Ursula argues back
convincingly, 'You want me to be a mere *thing* for you'. And when
she talks it over with Gudrun, her sister backs her up by saying he
just wants his ideas fulfilled; he has picked on her to live out his idea
of woman – which is all too true. But there is reason on both sides.
Birkin still laughs at Ursula's argument, saying that her 'Do you love
me?' question, is really a command like saying 'Yield knave, or die';
that she wanted 'to drink him down, like a life draught . . . She
believed that love was everything' (WL, p. 283). Also, when Gerald
and Gudrun try to work out a relationship, based more on the old
social order, we are shown in Gudrun just what that female lust for
possession is, 'One of them must triumph over the other. Which
should it be?' implying that Gudrun was going to do her best to win.
Birkin's argument for a 'lovely state of free proud singleness', or his
reply to Ursula that he wanted her to trust herself so, so implicitly,
that she can let herself go, seems preferable.

Unfortunately we never see how Birkin and Ursula work it out:
we leave them at the end of the novel, embarking on life together,
with a feeling of dread for them. But then Lawrence did not know

any more himself. He had not travelled that far along the road himself with Frieda. How was he to know? Later in his life, he continues the theory with the same hope, optimism and energy, through the characters of Connie Chatterley and Parkin in *John Thomas and Lady Jane*. Again the argument is for erotic union, for a love that is at once all-committing and freeing enough for individual growth. This time it is Connie who expresses the theory. It is Connie who says she recognises the idea of eternal love, but that the reality of marriage is so stultifying. 'Let there be permanency if it happens so. But let there be no conventional permanency especially in emotional or passional relationships' (JTLJ, p. 154). She plans out for herself and Parkin a life where they live in separate places, 'you'd find me a burden and a strain on you, if I was there morning, noon and night'. She tells him she does not believe in living together. That is what ruins marriage, the boredom, the burden.

It is in *John Thomas and Lady Jane* that we see one of Lawrence's recurring images for modern marriage: that of the ships grappled together, travelling in the same direction, but apart. 'Grapple the two vessels together, lash them side by side, and the first storm will squash them to pieces. That is marriage in the bad weather of modern civilisation. But leave the two vessels apart, each according to its own skill and power, and an unseen life force connects them, a magnetism which cannot be forced' (JTLJ, p. 302). How many modern people see their relationships in those terms today? A great many I am sure.

The steps Lawrence took to reach this stage of thinking can be traced through the early novels. The young Lawrence had only the lives of people close to him with which to compare his own, in particular that of his mother, about whose marriage he writes (in *The White Peacock*) 'a woman who finds her romance has been a temporary tale'. The early novels are full of examples of bad marriages; Lettie and Leslie, and then George and Meg, though George tries to reason himself into the relationship he has with Meg. It is one of those stable relationships, that Lawrence later described as good for companionship but not the stuff of real marriage: without spark or adventure. George says, 'And Meg's lovely. I can have her without trembling, she's full of soothing and comfort . . . all restfulness in one another'. Later, the marriage is shown to give George so little that he is a wreck of a man, fallen on drink and despair.

Paul Morel takes us through Lawrence's own paces, a demanding young man wanting a lot out of love and marriage and finding himself isolated in his community for asking such things. With Miriam, he tries. But she is too tradition-bound, unable to release herself for an erotic adventure, being restricted by the constraints of needing the social convention of marriage. In his famous letter to her, Paul says cruelly, 'You are a nun. I have given you what I would give a holy nun – as a mystic monk to a mystic nun . . . If people marry, they must live together as affectionate humans, who may be commonplace with each other without feeling awkward – not as two souls. So I feel it'. And talking himself out of his relationship with her, floundering in a sea of his own desires, desperate for sexual love, but at the same time frightened of the trap of it, he reasons, 'Marriage was for life . . . He did not feel he wanted marriage with Miriam . . . it was a strong desire battling with a still stronger shyness and virginity. It seemed as if virginity were a positive force, which fought and won in both of them' (SL, p. 340). Young Paul, however, has watched his parents' own marriage and though he knows of his mother's unhappiness now, he can perceive the energy and power that brought the two people together. '. . . with my father, at first, I'm sure she had the real thing. She knows; she has been there . . . once it has happened to you, you can go on with anything and ripen . . . the something big and intense that changes you when you really come together with somebody else. It almost seems to fertilise your soul and make it that you can go on and mature' (SL, pp. 386–7). Miriam said he was seeking a 'sort of baptism of fire in passion'. Strangely enough, if the real Jessie Chambers did say that to the real Bert Lawrence, he did find just that, later on.

Even with Clara, with whom Paul first finds the delights of true sexuality and a free woman who can indulge his young man's desires while not demanding complete possession of him, Paul can see quite clearly that he has to move on yet further before he finds the relationship that will satisfy him. 'They would have to part sooner or later. Even if they married, and were faithful to each other, still he would have to leave her, go on alone, and she would only have to attend to him when he came home. But it was not possible. Each wanted a mate to go side by side with' (SL, p. 439).

There is a change, however, in the middle phase of Lawrence's writing, from this straightforward idealism about relationship and marriage. The novels that deal with people of western civilisations testing themselves out in primitive societies – such as *The Lost Girl* and *The Plumed Serpent* – bring in more complex arguments that have confounded the feminists and turned the angry voice on Lawrence for seeming to demand the passive submission of woman to man. The complexity is caused by Lawrence's turning against western, civilised, educated nations and peoples – turning at the same time, symbolically, against similar women (rather than men). If these women are to find the ultimate marriage and relationship, he argues in these novels, they must give up their independent stance, their strong will, and submit, not so much to men, but to men who symbolise the primitive instinctual forces. The discussion cannot be seen strictly in terms of men versus women, if we bear in mind the influence on Lawrence of the intellectuals from Munich, who argued for the feminine state, for instinct and the primitive, above knowledge, or science, who argued for mythology and a way of life that was opposed to the forces of reason. Some of the passivity and submission in these women is a representation of the feminine state he approved of during this time of his travels away from England.

To some degree, Lawrence had again turned to this way of thinking after his own experience of life with Frieda. Their quarrelsome relationship had not settled down, and what had started out as an optimistic venture had, more and more, left Lawrence exhausted and lacking in confidence. It is likely that he was impotent for many of those years of their travels together, and that Frieda was capable of hurting his masculine pride, either with other men or just by her cutting tongue. Frieda was not a gentle, quiet woman. She was a product of the modern age, educated, full of self-will, independent and not likely to take nonsense from her husband just because he was a man. The fact that he was able to return to his optimistic, hedonistic theories at the end of his life, in the novels that became *Lady Chatterley's Lover*, indicates, however, that he never completely lost his faith in the man–woman relationship. Whatever you feel, from the feminist side, there is still strong evidence to support Lawrence's primitive theories. What westernised people need to do to find the 'ultimate marriage' is indeed to submit, become passive, give in to the dark instinctual forces in themselves. Recalling his fascination with duality, *The Lost Girl* and *The Plumed Serpent* draw upon the triumph of the bowels over the breast, the loins over the face. This is the ultimate expression of the feminine mode of being.

Alvina, in her relationship with Cicio, gives in not only to Cicio as a man, but to the force of Italian culture, rich, florid and abundant, over the deathliness of a Midlands life for young women like herself.

Her future there was doomed to be dry, sterile and spinsterish. By throwing in her lot with Cicio, she gains uncertainty, but with it passion, adventure and fire. In the chapter called 'Alvina comes Alive', Lawrence describes her submissiveness to Cicio, regarding Alvina as his victim. This is the death of the individual, described in theory by Birkin. It is a fascinating passage:

> But in his eyes, which kept hers, there was a dark flicker of ascendancy. He was going to triumph over her. She knew it. And her soul sank, as if it sank out of her body . . . left her there powerless, soulless . . . she looked up at him, like a victim . . .
>
> 'You love me? Yes? – Yes?' he said, in a voice that seemed like a palpable contact on her.
>
> 'Yes', she whispered involuntarily, soulless, like a victim. He put his arm round her, subtly, and lifted her . . . and smiling, he kissed her, delicately, with a certain finesse of knowledge. She moaned in spirit, in his arms, felt herself dead, dead.
>
> . . . She turned, slipped past, ran indoors and upstairs to the little bare bedroom she had made her own. She locked the door and kneeled down on the floor, bowing down her head to her knees in a paroxysm on the floor. In a paroxysm – because she loved him . . . It was far more like pain, like agony, than like joy . . . And taking a pillow from the bed, she crushed it against herself and swayed herself unconsciously, in her orgasm of unbearable feeling. Right in her bowels she felt it – the terrible, unbearable feeling (LG, pp. 212–13).

It is a very strong passage of sexuality and emotion – pure and unadulterated. It is also very bold – though maybe contemporary readers did not realise this as they did with Lady Chatterley – because Alvina is described as masturbating herself to orgasm, and writhing in the typical female fantasy of reliving a powerful sexual experience, which specialists now call the 'flashback' form of fantasy. Who can deny Alvina this release? Who can say it is worse to love a man like a victim, than to lose one's independence to a man? It is where Lawrence stumbled over his own theories. For the danger of aiming for the perfect passion, eroticism, deepest feelings is that the balance or 'equilibrium' is hard to maintain, and the likelihood is that one would go over the top. Also, the reality of the feminine mode of being is that it is dark, instinctive, irrational, and heavily emotional; deep, intense and completely submissive to a power stronger than its own. It is what has, to some degree, doomed women to a life of servitude over the centuries, and, at the same time, given them an extra dimension of experience that most men have never had.

Kate Leslie, in *The Plumed Serpent*, is older than Alvina and has taken herself to a primitive land in search of something deeper and more forceful in her rather stale life. Kate is at once attracted to, and repelled by, Cipriano and his proposal of marriage to her:

> 'Get used to it', he said, ' . . . that there must be a bit of fear, and a bit of horror in your life. And marry me, and you will find many things that are not horror' . . . She was breathless with amazement, because he had made her see the physical possibility of marrying him: a thing she had never even glimpsed before. But surely, surely, it would not be *herself* who could marry him. It would be some curious female within her, whom she did not know and did not own (PS, p. 249).

Kate, in thinking about what marriage means to her, and what Cipriano's proposal means in the light of that, is rather like Ursula, a few years on, pondering Birkin's odd proposition: 'I feel he just wants something of me; and perhaps I just want something of him. But he would never meet me . . . He would come to take something from me and I should have to let him. And I don't want merely that. I want a man who will come half-way, just half-way, to meet me' (PS, p. 284). So says Kate, just as Ursula felt. But both women are proved wrong by the men, who point out that it is just female will battling for a win. It is Don Ramon who voices the ideas for Kate to absorb:

> But I am nauseated with humanity and the human will: even with my own will. I have realised that *my will*, no matter how intelligent I am, is only another nuisance on the face of the earth, once I start exerting it. And other people's *wills* are even worse . . . Kate listened in silence. She knew the road he had gone, but she herself had not yet come to the end of it. As yet she was still strong in the pride of her own – her very own *will* (PS, pp. 80–1).

Kate, at the end of the novel, decides to stay. That means she stays on Cipriano's terms, perhaps rather unconvincingly, but we cannot help but applaud her for her courage – after all, to go back to England, alone, would be the more sterile, cowardly, decision. What sort of life she had there is left to anybody's imagination, unfortunately.

The other two novels of that middle period, *Aaron's Rod* and *Kangaroo*, both express more cynicism with the man–woman relationship, and more hostility towards women. Aaron, a rather lost, wandering figure, trying to find himself as a man, is given the voice of anti-love, and marriage, a man who has found the close intense man–woman relationship too stultifying:

> I wanted to have a bit of free room round me – to loose myself. . . I wanted fresh air . . . A breath of fresh air, by myself. I felt forced to love. I feel if I go back home now, I shall be *forced* – forced to love – or care – or something . . . She's made up her mind she loves me, and she's not going to let me off . . . I shall never love anybody else. But I'm damned if I want to go on being a lover, to her or anybody (AR, p. 83).

This is Lawrence expressing the other side of the coin. Where women go for the lust of possession, they become altogether too cloying and stultifying. It is part of a different period of Lawrence's life which I will come to later. The other book, *Kangaroo*, written hastily while Lawrence and Frieda were in Australia, again explores themes of men and masculinity, defends marriage rather more than *Aaron's Rod*, and repeats one of Lawrence's images about the ships sailing side by side on their own momentum, because once they are lashed together that is the end:

> Two ships may sail together to the world's end. But lock them together in mid-ocean and try to steer both with one rudder, and they will smash one another to bits. So it is when one individual seeks absolutely to love, or trust, another . . . And yet, love is the greatest thing between human beings, men and women, men and men, women and women, when it is love, when it happens. But when human love starts out to lock individuals together, it is just courting disaster. Man-and-woman love is a disaster nowadays (K, p. 220).

Lawrence says this as if signing off. Surprising, therefore, that he was able to write *Lady Chaterley's Lover* after this diversion into the field of alternatives: in which he has been looking for friendship and love between the same sex, to take the pressure off the opposite sex.

6   Sexuality and Women

'The celebration of sexual passion for which the book is so renowned is largely a celebration of the penis of Oliver Mellors, gamekeeper and social prophet' (KM, p. 238). – Kate Millett writing in her vitriolic attack on Lawrence in *Sexual Politics*. Ms Millett's essay on Lawrence can be read with interest, as few women have attempted critical studies of Lawrence. I wanted to know what her deep feelings were, but all I came away with was a feeling of anger and hostility parallel, though opposite, to her own, that someone could so misread Lawrence's works, so misrepresent him as a man of ideas. Millett's work of criticism shows a determination to read one point of view into the novels. We take opposite points of view: Lawrence, to me, treats female sexuality with an originality and a sense of excitement that no man had ever brought to it before. Lawrence, to my mind, was the first novelist to show, probably better than any female novelist ever had, the strength and power of a woman's feelings, sexual and erotic, by showing his women characters in relationship with men they loved passionately. Here is liberation of women, in a subtle fashion. Here is woman saying openly that she is a sexual being, she enjoys sensuality and sexuality, and that she enjoys fucking – with men.

Lawrence's place in the history of writing about sexuality is loosely linked with what has been discussed as his possible connection with Edward Carpenter. Whether or not he knew directly of Carpenter's works, through the agency of Alice Dax, remains a mystery. But the connections run firm. Lawrence and Carpenter had a common passionate desire to understand their own psychology, relating to their inner conflicts. Delavenay quotes one Irene Clephane, in a criticism of Carpenter's *Love's Coming of Age* – written after Lawrence's death – in *Towards Sex Freedom* (1935) on the significance of Carpenter's collection of essays. Carpenter lived, she wrote, in a world 'ashamed to discuss the intimacies of sex relationships, either verbally or in print'. His own attitude was 'a new outlook on sex as something to be accepted and enjoyed instead of repressed and feared' (EC, p. 9). Lawrence would have been an impressionable young man in the years when Carpenter's ideas were first becoming known (1905–18), fighting in his own mind the mental attitudes of late- and post-Victorian socialist England in the Midlands. Those Victorian ideas controlled not only the political and economic dependence of the individual, but the moral constraints of society as well. Liberation of the individual became the ethos of *avant- garde* thinkers of the age, as the writers of Orage's *The New Age* were keen to explore.

Edward Carpenter's ideas were anti-Victorian, longing for a freer, more human society, in which men and women were acknowledged as individuals and in which sexuality in all its forms, was openly recognised. *Love's Coming of Age* was of course repressed and refused publication till 1902, because of its homosexual content; typical of the age which condemned Oscar Wilde for homosexuality in 1895. Interesting, too, is the fact that both Carpenter and Lawrence were prosecuted for obscenity in the same year, 1915, for producing *The Intermediate Sex* and *The Rainbow*. Enid Hilton (daughter of William and Sallie Hopkin of Eastwood) has written of Lawrence that he would not accept homosexuality himself, at least not openly, because there was still much of the class-imposed morality about him, even while he was trying to free England from the constricting coils of hush-hush in other ways.

But homosexuality, and its exposure in public, was really the key to the opening up of all talk of sexuality. With an acceptance of homosexuality, came an acceptance of female sexuality too. Edward Carpenter was a central figure in the movement for sexual freedom, as was Havelock Ellis. One of their ideas was to educate the public to a more liberal attitude to sex and marriage, by stating that the reproduction of the race is not the primary object of love or sex. Once you take reproduction out of sex then you liberate women to a positive attitude towards their own sexuality. Carpenter's message was, 'taking all together I think it may fairly be said that the prime object of Sex is *union*, the physical union as the allegory and expression of the real union, and that generation is a secondary object or result of this union' (EC, p. 93). Carpenter, like Lawrence, saw sex as an exchange of cells between male and female. Again, like Lawrence he advocated sex in the open air, in touch with the abundance of nature. Carpenter, the homosexual, significantly fought most strongly for the emancipation of woman in all things sexual.

Carpenter saw the traditional stereotype of man (that is, the male) as a half-grown being, who had relegated women to the boudoir or harem, or to a life of drudgery. Whereas woman, he thought, should be seen as 'his guide in sexual matters'. In *Love's Coming of Age*, he says that 'what woman most needs today, is a basis for independence of her life, to dispose of herself and of her sex perfectly freely'. He, too, like Lawrence, regretted the repression of the English language, that it had been confined in literature since the nineteenth century, 'within the stifling atmosphere of the drawing room' (EC, p. 175). He wanted to bring back words that were 'the coarse, the concrete, the vulgar and the physiologial side in human life and passion' (EC, p. 176).

By the time Lawrence's voice was being heard, several years later, his views struck similar notes. His attitude toward the writing about sex is well known, from letters and essays. In 'A Propos of *Lady Chatterley's Lover*', he says he is thinking about 'sex, fully, completely, honestly and cleanly', regarding both men and women. 'It means having a proper reverence for sex, and a proper awe of the body's strange experiences' (P. p. 510). In a letter of April 1927 he wrote, 'I am in a quandary about my novel, *Lady Chatterley's Lover*. It's what the world would call very improper. But you know it's not really improper – I always labour at the same thing, to make the sex relation valid and precious, instead of shameful. This novel is the furthest I've gone. To me, it is beautiful and tender and frail as the naked self is, and I shrink very much from even having it typed' (L, 12 April 1927). He decided in his own way to call it *Tenderness*, a title that has caused a lot of anti-Lawrence mirth, but which bears him out. A letter the following year, in December 1928, to Lady Ottoline Morrell, his influential friend and not a lover but a lady interested in new ideas, goes even further, showing how he felt about language, and about open honesty towards sex – the fact he could write this to Lady Ottoline shows how much he believed in the ideas himself:

About Lady Chatterley – you mustn't think I advocate perpetual sex. Far from it. Nothing nauseates me more than promiscuous sex in and out of season. But I want, with Lady Chatterley, to make an adjustment in consciousness to the basic physical realities. I realise that one of the reasons why the commonpeople often keep or kept – the good natural glow of life, just warm life, longer than educated people, was because it was still possible for them to say —— or —— without either a shudder or a sensation. If a man had been able to say to you when you were young and in love: an' if tha shits, an' if tha pisses, I' glad, I shouldna want a woman who couldna shit nor piss – surely it would have been a liberation to you, and it would have helped keep your heart warm' (L, 28 December 1928).

Ironically, of course, the edition of the Letters did not permit the publication of those words deemed so important by Lawrence.

Martin Green describes some of the difficulties Lawrence, the man, found in living out and writing about his theories. His attitude towards sex, and women, was all part of his general attitude towards letting women take over, letting himself explore the feminine side of life. Ultimately, its implications were huge, for they reversed the whole patriarchal pattern. 'In Lawrence's version of the world of Women, for example, it is the women who are the sexual agents and the men who are called upon to surrender to them . . . Thus it is Anna Brangwen who undresses and caresses Will' (MG, p. 78). In the poems, we see what happened in his own life when he gave Frieda this power. She took possession of him and reduced him to the role of sexual object for herself. 'The resentment was . . . part of the price that had to be paid for the bold reversal of patriarchal patterns of sexuality that accompanied the new doctrine or Eros' (MG, p. 78) – that is, the resentment was result of conflict, not the crass attitude of a chauvinist male as depicted by Kate Millett.

From the novels, the most basic difference in Lawrence's attitude towards women and their sexuality is, as Martin Green says, that it is the women who are shown as agents of sex. The action comes from them, rather than from the men. Even back in his early writings, when the ideas were not fully worked out, we find Miriam, the virgin queen of *Sons and Lovers,* expressing some of the modern woman's feeling: 'She loved him absorbedly. She wanted to run her hands down his sides. She always wanted to embrace him, so long as he did not want her . . . She did not seem to realise *him* in all this. He might have been an object' (SL, p. 233). Paul, for Miriam, is a sex-object – quite a reversal of thinking for those days.

By the time Paul meets Clara, we are learning some of his, and Lawrence's, attitudes towards women. Far from Millett's theory that the whole of Lawrence's writings are to 'celebrate the penis', Lawrence manages to evoke some of the wonder he obviously felt for the female form. Clara is described. 'Her neck gave him a sharp pang, such a beautiful thing . . . Her breasts swung slightly in her blouse . . . she wore no stays. Suddenly, without knowing, he was scattering a handful of cowslips over her hair and neck' (SL, p. 292). Later when they were out walking together, 'She stood on top of the stile . . . Then she leaped. Her breast came against his; he held her, and covered her faces with kisses . . . His finger-tips felt the rocking of her breast' (SL, p. 375).

Paul is going through the conflicts of a young man. He knows he is interested in girls for sex, he knows he should not be – after all he was brought up in the puritanical Midlands – and sometimes his passions torture him:

> . . . A good many of the nicest men he knew were like himself, bound in by their own virginity . . . They were so sensitive to their women that they would go without them for ever rather than do them a hurt, an injustice. Being the sons of mothers whose husbands had blundered rather brutally through their feminine sanctities . . . they could easier deny themselves than incur any reproach from a woman; for a woman was like their mother, and they were full of the sense of their mother (SL, p. 341).

Yet feminist critics deny Lawrence's sensitivity towards women!

Millett in fact makes many judgements of Lawrence and sex; saying that for him, in sex, 'ladies don't move' and that he had borrowed Freud's theories of female passivity and male activity, 'and doubtless found them very convenient' (NM, p. 240). She quotes his use of adjectives to describe the male phallus, as 'proud', 'lordly', 'lovely', 'terrifying', and 'strange'. In his defence, we have to look no further than this same scene between Paul and Clara, in *Sons and Lovers,* a novel Lawrence wrote as a very young man, long before he began *Lady Chatterley's Lover* and really worked out his ideas about the novel and sex. Clara is described as wanting to have sex with him: 'She stood letting him adore her and tremble with joy of her . . . it made her glad. It made her feel erect and proud again . . . she had been cheapened. Now she radiated with joy and pride again' (SL, p. 412). Note the type of adjectives Lawrence employs in describing the woman in action: 'erect', 'proud', and even 'radiating' – all very positive, active, and nothing to do with the stereotype of female passivity. Needless to say, Lawrence could not have 'borrowed' from Freud; as we have already seen, Freud was only an embryonic influence on Lawrence. What was more of an influence was the general atmosphere of ideas and reversal of traditional thinking on men, women, and sex.

In *The Rainbow*, it is the Brangwen women, forever looking outward, who take over in all things sexual, who threaten to control, dominate and use men as sex objects. Lydia, with her Tom, is the first to dictate to a man how he should treat her. 'You don't make it good between us any more, you are not interested. You do not make me want you', she cries, then later, we see just how powerful she is:

> And she put her arms round him as he stood before her, round his thighs, pressing him against her breast. And her hands on him seemed to reveal to him the mould of his own nakedness, he was passionately lovely to himself . . . He suffered from the compulsion to her. She was the awful unknown . . . She waited for him to meet her, not to bow before her and serve her. She wanted his active participation, not his submission (R, pp. 94–5).

Through Lydia we see a complete role reversal – her man only learns of sexuality through her and becomes passive to her active. It is Tom who is being described as 'submissive'.

Daughter Anna, forerunner of Ursula, in her relationship with Will always acts first; always feels, and makes the moves. If anyone wanted to find active imagery for sexual activity, they need look no further: 'Suddenly she had her arms round him, was clinging close to him, cleaving her body against his, and crying, in a whispering, whimpering sound. "Will, I love you, I love you, Will, I love you." It sounded as if it were tearing her' (R, p. 118). Will is so much in her hands that he is described as being completely transformed by love for her, 'He was translated with gladness to be in her hands'. Anna is more the devil than Will: she knows how to play him, how to get the man out of him, make him the 'active participant'. She provokes, taunts and plays wilful games with him:

> So she loved him and caressed him and roused him like a hawk, till he was keen and instant, but without tenderness . . . If she imitated the pathetic plover running plaintive to him, that was part of the game . . . she dashed at him and threw him from his station savagely, she goaded him from his keen dignity of a male, she harassed him from his unperturbed pride, till he was mad with rage (R, pp. 62–3).

Ursula, with Skrebensky, is also described as the active one in lovemaking; she 'hung close to him', 'pressed herself', 'she clung at the core of him', 'her lips holding open the very bottommost source of him'. And she knows how much she wants the sex with him, though she does feel a mixture of 'shame and bliss' (R, p. 304).

Not all Lawrence's novels are explicit about sex. However, one of the lesser-known ones contains some of the most powerful, if bizarre, writings about female sexuality. Kate Millett picks on this as the ultimate example of Lawrentian chauvinism, showing how sadistic the author is in his attitudes towards women (NM, p. 240). Yet *The Plumed Serpent*, as we have already seen, to some degree contains some of Lawrence's most complicated ideas on men and women, the duality of love, and the essence of the conflict between the natural woman and the product of western civilisation. Kate Leslie is an independent, educated, self-motivated woman. She meets, in Don Cipriano, more than her match. In sex, Cipriano conducts what could be described as the most sadistic act against a woman – he withholds her orgasm. However, another way of looking at Cipriano's act is to see it as a means of educating Kate in traditionally eastern values to be slower, to accept the flow of natural sex, not to be struggling and striving for the self-motivated orgasm that Lawrence knew was the drive of modern western woman – the masterbatory orgasm. Take what Cipriano does as you will, Millett is wrong in assuming that Lawrence finds woman's activity in sex, her orgasm, as something repulsive. Far from it. He describes in detail the extremely active movements of the woman in ecstasy:

> She realised, almost with wonder, the death in her of the Aphrodite of the foam: the seething, frictional, ecstatic Aphrodite. By a swift dark instinct, Cipriano drew away from this in her. When, in their love, it came back to her, the seething electric female ecstasy, which knows such spasms of delirium, he recoiled from her. It was what she used to call her 'satisfaction'. She had loved Joachim for this, that again, and again, and again he could give her this orgiastic 'satisfaction', in spasms that made her cry aloud . . . And she, as she lay, would realise the worthlessness of this foam-effervescence, its strange externality to her. It seemed to come upon her from without, not from within. And succeeding the first moment of disappointment, when this sort of 'satisfaction' was denied her, came the knowledge that she did

not really want it, that it was really nauseous to her.

And he, in his dark, hot silence would bring her back to the new, soft, heavy, hot flow, when she was like a fountain gushing noiseless and with urgent softness from the volcanic deeps. Then she was open to him soft and hot, yet gushing with a noiseless soft power. And there was no such thing as conscious 'satisfaction'. What happened was dark and untellable. So different from the beak-like friction of Aphrodite of the foam . . . (PS, p. 439).

Electric, ecstatic, writhing, and foaming – the Lawrence woman is not exactly passive in sex.

It is Connie Chatterley who best underlines Lawrence's attitude towards female sexuality. Connie is foremost a privileged woman in that she is allowed to *adore* the male body. Rather than see this as a male narcissitic pride in loving oneself, I would prefer to think that, to Lawrence, it was a breakthrough – to give woman the possibility of adoring man. Time and again male novelists, including Lawrence, have written about man smitten by the sight of female breasts, flesh, hair and, though not often in his day, lower regions, but how often had woman – who by Victorian standards was not supposed to enjoy sex – been able to admit her own predilections?

[Connie] The white torso of the man had seemed so beautiful to her, opening on the gloom. The white, firm, divine body, with its silky ripple, the white arch of life, as it bent forward over the water, seemed, she could not help it, of the world of gods . . . she had seen beauty, and beauty alive . . . A great soothing came over her heart, along with the feeling of worship. The sudden sense of pure beauty, beauty that was active and alive, had put worship in her heart again (JTLJ, p. 51).

Such writing does not imprison women in passivity, but frees them to an equal appreciation of the male nude form, such as had long been enjoyed by men of women, in both art and life.

In *Lady Chatterley's Lover*, or *John Thomas and Lady Jane*, Lawrence is trying to write about his theory of the 'phallic consciousness' related to human sexuality. The first thing to accept about the phrase is that, in taking the word 'phallic' too literally, as meaning just male sexuality, you run the danger of misinterpreting his full intent. Lawrence did see the phallus as the vital connection between the life force of man and that of woman. But then, like any two parts, the one is rendered inactive and inert without the other. The 'phallic consciousness' is the term used to mean an awareness, an opening up to, the forces of deep, instinctual sexuality, not a holding back to the mental form of sex he saw in western society, that he calls 'sex in the head'. In a letter to Curtis Brown, his agent, in March 1928, he wrote, trying to explain:

> I believe in the phallic consciousness, as against the irritable cerebral consciousness we're afflicted with: and anybody who calls my novel a dirty sexual novel is a liar. It's not even a sexual novel, it's phallic. Sex is a thing that exists in the head, its reactions are cerebral, and its processes mental. Whereas the phallic reality is warm and spontaneous – but basta' (L, 15 March 1928).

When Lawrence is writing about his worries in getting the novel published, he explains further: 'I must bring out the book complete. It is – in the latter half at least – a phallic novel, but tender and delicate. You know I believe in the phallic reality and the phallic consciousness: as distinct from our irritable cerebral consciousness today. That's why I do the book – and it's not just *sex*. Sex alas is one of the worst phenomena of today: all cerebral reaction, the whole thing worked from mental processes and itch, and not a bit of the real phallic insouciance and spontaneity. But in my novel there is.'

The interesting fact is that the eroticism of the novel is hers; the urge for sex is mostly Connie's – or at least seen through the woman's needs and desires. It is Connie who perceives the 'phallic spontaneity'. 'Then he took her and laid her down, wasting no time, breaking her underclothing in his urgency. And her will seemed to have left her entirely. And then, something awoke in her. Strange, thrilling sensation, that she had never known before woke up where he was within her, in wild thrills like wild, wild bells . . . But it was over too soon, too soon! She clung to him in a sort of fear . . . It would be too, too soon lost' (JTLJ, p. 133). The phallis, even, is described as hers, 'The man, the mere man, with his independent soul and personality . . . He was but a temple servant, the guardian and keeper of the bright phallus, which was hers, her own' (JTLJ, p. 136).

The trouble with feminist critics is that anything that passes for celebration of the male can be read as denigration of the female. So, when Connie is loving the penis, loving the sex, admiring her man, it has been read as meaning that Lawrence is not considering her wishes. Yet Connie is the active one; she is the participant, lover, doer and, of the two, the one with the most expressed feelings. We should give Lawrence credit, in Carpenter-type terms, for emancipating Connie so she can simply wonder and enjoy 'fucking'.

> She clung to him, and caressed him, and felt his phallus rise against her. 'I love it', she said, quivering, and feeling the rapid thrills go through her loins, 'I love it when he rises like that, so proud. It's the only time when I feel there is nothing *really* to be afraid of, from all over the world of people. They seem so insignificant. I love it when he comes in to me!' (JTLJ, p. 264).

After all, if Connie is going to enjoy heterosexual intercourse, then she has to be able to enjoy the man, and the look and feel of him.

Lawrence is explicit about Connie's former sex life. He had experienced other women in his own life, as well as Frieda, and knew what modern women were like. He knew they liked sex, and arranged their own orgasms. This side of women is the one he draws on for the hostility Parkin or Mellors feel to women. The way women had learned to use men as sex objects, a trend which continues even more strongly today, upset the traditional man in Lawrence.

> A woman could take a man without really giving herself away . . . she only had to hold herself back in sexual intercourse, and let him finish and expend himself without herself coming to the crisis; and then she could prolong the connection and achieve her orgasm and her crisis while he was merely her tool (LCL, p. 8).

In *Lady Chatterley*, her previous affair with Michael is described thus: '. . . she soon learned to hold him, to keep him there inside her when his crisis was over . . . wildly, passionately active, coming to her own crisis. And as he felt the frenzy of her achieving her own orgasmic satisfaction from his hard, erect passivity, he had a curious sense of pride and satisfaction' (LCL, p. 31).

Through Mellors, Connie learns a different attitude towards man, and towards sex. She learns to admit the dark, deep, animal instincts and recognises the force and power within both their bodies. It necessitates her submission and her powerlessness, if she is to find such passion, however:

He too had bared the front part of his body and she felt his naked flesh against her as he came into her . . . But it was over too soon, too soon, and she could no longer force her own conclusion with her own activity . . . While all her womb was open and soft, and softly clamouring, like a sea-anenome under the tide, clamouring for him to come in again and make a fulfilment for her. She clung to him unconsious in passion, and he never quite slipped from her, and she felt the soft bud of him within her stirring, and strange rhythms flushing up into her with a strange rhythmic growing motion, swelling and swelling till it filled all her cleaving consciousness . . . And they lay and knew nothing, not even of each other, both lost (LCL, pp. 138–9).

Kate Millett accuses Lawrence of scarcely describing the female genital organs, thus showing his negative feelings towards women. Again, I would rather argue in his defence, that perhaps even Lawrence knew little of the real beauty of female parts – who can tell what, in his own life, he had actually seen. But then, Mellors is given time to adore Connie's body. One such passage touches the very essence of how a woman would see her own body as beautiful:

At that moment he felt a sheer love for the woman. He kissed her belly and her mound of Venus, to kiss close to the womb and the foetus within the womb . . . And he went into her softly, feeling the stream of tenderness flowing in release from his bowels to hers, the bowels of compassion kindled between them . . . 'I stand for the touch of bodily awareness between human beings', he said to himself, 'and the touch of tenderness. And she is my mate . . . Thank God I've got a woman! Thank God I've got a woman who is with me, and tender and aware of me. Thank God she's not a bully, nor a fool. Thank God, she's a tender, aware woman'. And as his seed sprang in her, his soul sprang towards her too, in the creative act that is far more than procreative (LCL, p. 292).

The final words should go to Connie, reflecting about the male body. This is ultimately the modern woman's point of view. This is the attitude all those other Lawrence women, his mother, Miriam, Clara, Lydia, Anna, Ursula and Kate, would have loved to have had the chance to express too. For woman, in full flood of adoration, is woman given potency. She is choosing to love, rather than to be the passive object of love. I quote in full because I find it personally so beautiful:

> A man! The strange potency of manhood upon her! Her hands strayed over him, still a little afraid. Afraid of that strange, hostile, slightly repulsive thing that he had been to her, a man . . . How beautiful he felt, how pure in tissue! How lovely, how lovely, strong, and yet pure and delicate, such stillness of the sensitive body! . . . Her hands came timorously down his back, to the soft, smallish globes of the buttocks. Beauty! What beauty! . . . The life within life, the sheer warm, potent loveliness. And the strange weight of the balls between his legs! What a mystery! What a strange heavy weight of mystery that could lie soft and heavy in one's hand! The roots, root of all that is lovely, the primeval root of all full beauty . . . she felt again the slow, momentous, surging rise of the phallus again, the other power. And her heart melted out with a kind of awe (LCL, p. 182).

7 Homosexuality

It has become fashionable to say that Lawrence was really a homosexual, as if somehow that explains his sometimes confused attitude towards women. Or, more narrowly, that that explains his dislike of women. But Lawrence was no hater of women. He took femaleness and the female point of view very seriously, to the extent that he wanted to explore its relevance in the modern world, and its significance as an element of maleness. What we could deduce is that Lawrence may indeed have suffered from repressed homosexuality; but it is more likely that he was one of the newer breed of 'intersexuals', as defined by Edward Carpenter, an androgynous person struggling with the conflicts inside him. Above all, we have to remember, whether it was from his own psychological needs, or because of the social pressures of his time, Lawrence wanted to be a 'real' man, and a manly one at that – not a homosexual.

His excursion into the realms of male friendship, however, should be of great interest to modern readers, who in recent years have experienced a rediscovery of friendship between women. Lawrence talks about men coming together with men, finding love and brotherhood, in very similar terms to those used by women in the sixties and seventies. The value he places on man-to-man friendship is no more or less than many a late twentieth-century feminist has tried to describe. To Lawrence the love between man and woman, in all its intensity, is still not enough for the individual soul – he wanted love between men too, but he was not sure how to go about it. In his own life, as is evident from the book *Son of Mother* (by John Middleton Murry) and from biographies of Lawrence, his friendship with Middleton Murry was the inspiration for such ideas, and the frustration of them, at one and the same time.

In later life, the force of his feelings about women had become thwarted and the same tensions that made up his vision of the duality in relationships between man and woman had teetered over the top as he began to see woman as the great threat – even to the extent of hating them, for the very things he had loved in them only a few years previously. It would still be foolish to deduce that Lawrence, who probably became impotent in his relations with Frieda as he became older and more unhealthy, formed these theories only as a jaded, bitter, sick, middle-aged man. He had had the roots of this other side of his vision in his early, optimistic, idealistic, youth too.

The first instance, at least the first recorded one, of Lawrence's infatuation with a male friend came through his relationship with Jessie Chambers. It was her brother Alan Chambers who brought out those feelings in the young Lawrence. In the novels *The White Peacock* and *Sons and Lovers* there is indeed plenty of evidence of such feelings. Edgar, in *Sons and Lovers,* and George Sexton, in *The White Peacock,* were the focal points of Lawrence's young vision of male friendship. As his biographer, Harry Moore, writes, 'for the original of George and Edgar he must have felt something for which the best name is the simple one of love'. But then, as he goes on to say, 'such an emotion at the time of adolescence is neither infrequent nor "unnatural" as the world learned somewhere between Freud and Kinsey' (PL, p. 80).

In a letter to Blanche Jennings, in 1908, Lawrence wrote

> You tell me I have no male friends. The man I have been working with in the hay is the original of my George lacking, alas, the other's subtlety of sympathetic discrimination which lent him his nobility. But I am very fond of my friend, and he of me. Sometimes, often, he is gentle as a woman towards me. It seems my men friends are all alike, they make themselves, on the whole, soft-mannered towards me; they defer to me also. You are right. I value the friendship of men more than that of women . . . But better a woman vibrating with incoherent hum than a man altogether dumb, eh? So to make a Jonathan for me, it would take the natures of ten men such as I know to complete the keyboard (PL, p. 83).

It does, however, have to be admitted that the actual instances of Lawrence's adulatory writing about men are many, and they are seen to ring with a glow that his writing about women often lacks. Here, he is able to write about beauty and love with no holds barred; when he is discussing women somehow it is always tempered by the reality of what the relationship could mean. George Sexton, in *The White Peacock*, obviously set the young Lawrence's blood stirring. The narrator is Cyril, who fortunately or unfortunately comes across as a weak, very wet individual, so the writing does not seem out of place. The Cyril/George friendship is a sideline to the main plot of the novel, the story of Lettie, George and Leslie. This is Cyril's description of George working in the fields: '. . . when I looked up, it was to see the motion of his limbs and his head, the rise and fall of his rhythmic body . . . We sat close together and watched the rain fall . . . It was at these times we formed the almost passionate attachment which later years slowly wore away' (WP, p. 253). So, was Lawrence homosexual? Most people who knew him believe not. Frieda wrote to Edward Gilbert in 1949, 'Murry and he had no "love affair". But he did not disbelieve in homosexuality' (PL, p. 84). If there was a homosexual spell in his life, she believed it lasted a short time in the First World War days in Cornwall. The most likely answer is that whatever Lawrence might have wanted, with his body, his mind would not have let him carry out. He was too much a Victorian.

Lawrence never acknowledged the homosexual Edward Carpenter, as writer or thinker. Sallie Hopkin's daughter, Enid Hilton, explained her reason why, in a letter to Emile Delavenay: 'The Carpenter writings were not acceptable – homosexuality was not acknowledged. I wonder if Lawrence preferred *not* to know Carpenter, publicly at least. He preferred his own twist to the theories of the other man . . . There was a streak of the Chapel-imposed morality about him, as with all of us of the period. He had that even whilst trying to free England from the constricting coils of hush-hush' (EC, pp. 40–1). Lawrence declared his antipathy, in fact, to the practice of homosexuality, in a letter to Bertrand Russell, in 1915, in which he declared his hatred of sodomy. He said that a challenging relationship with a woman is a creative relationship – but in male sodomy 'the man goes to the man to repeat this reaction on himself. It is a near form of masterbation' (PL, p. 86–7). His friend, Catherine Carswell, wrote of him in *The Savage Pilgrimage*, 'he cherished the deep longing to see revived a communion between man and man that should not lack its physical symbols'. He believed further that the recovery of 'true potency' and the restoration of 'health and happiness, between man and woman' depended upon a 'renewal of the sacredness between man and man' (PL, p. 85). Another late friend, the writer Richard Aldington, put Lawrence's homosexuality at 15 per cent and his heterosexuality at 85 per cent. Maybe one of his early female involvements, the independent and hard-headed woman Helen Corke, was able to understand him best. Helen Corke herself became homosexual and used the term 'Neutral Ground', for the title of her autobiography, describing the 'intermediate sexes'. In a television interview with Malcolm Muggeridge, in 1968, when she was 86, she described how she saw Lawrence in those days. He was, she thought, in the middle part of the spectrum of sex, which had its extremes, with the masculine and feminine at opposite ends, with an intermediate position which was 'that of some of our finest artists' (PL, p. 132).

From Lawrence's most autobiographical novel, *Sons and Lovers*, we can deduce that his love for his mother was out-of-the-ordinary, and that the several passages in other novels in which he describes one man rubbing another, in a sexual and motherly way, imply that Lawrence perhaps lived with the fantasy of being a woman who was loved by a man. The indications are there for anyone to make their own analysis. Paul, in *Sons and Lovers,* is startlingly open about his Oedipal affections:

> . . . bowing his head and hiding his eyes on her shoulder in misery. His mother kissed him a long, fervent kiss.
> 'My boy!' she said, in a voice trembling with passionate love.
> Without knowing, he gently stroked her face (SL, p. 262).

With his mother, for the day out in Lincoln, Paul says, 'You never mind my money', . . . 'You forget I'm a fellow taking his girl for an outing' (SL, p. 294). Later in the novel when Paul's sex problems become evident, Lawrence shows how over-identification with his mother led to problems with his own masculine identification *vis-à-vis* other women. 'They were so sensitive to their women . . . Being the sons of mothers whose husbands had blundered rather brutally through their feminine sanctities . . . for a woman was like their mother, and they were full of the sense of their mother' (SL, p. 341).

In other novels, Lawrence is more explicit about his sexual love for men – disguising it often as his theory of male friendship complementing marriage in novels as disparate as *Kangaroo* and *Aaron's Rod*. In *The White Peacock* there is a graphic description of a physical act of love between men which seems to express Lawrence's homosexual fantasy life; it involves the male love object, mother figure, touching or rubbing the body of the Lawrence figure – bringing to mind the virtues he had described, in the letter to Blanche Jennings, of a male friend who would be gentle and loving. The *White Peacock* scene occurs between George and Cyril in the chapter called 'A Poem on Friendship'. The words used are sexual, in a Lawrentian sense: 'bow to him', 'gentle manner', 'submitted', 'white fruitfulness of his form', 'rub me . . . as if I were a child', or 'a woman he loved and did not fear'. I will quote the passage in full as it is very important; and beautifully written:

> We stood and looked at each other as we rubbed ourselves dry. He was well proportioned, and naturally of handsome physique, heavily limbed. He laughed at me, telling me I was like one of Aubrey Beardsley's long, lean ugly fellows . . . But I had to give in, and bow to him, and he took on an indulgent, gentle manner. I laughed and submitted. For he knew not I admired the noble, white fruitfulness of his form . . .
>
> He saw I had forgotten to continue by rubbing, and laughing he took hold of me and began to rub me briskly, as if I were a child, or rather, a woman he loved and did not fear. I left myself quite limply in his hands, and, to get a better grip of me, be put his arms round me and pressed me against him, and the sweetness of the touch of our naked bodies one against the other was superb. It satisfied in some measure the vague, indecipherable yearning of my soul; and it was the same with him. When he had rubbed me all warm, he let me go, and we looked at each other with eyes of still laughter, and our love was perfect for a moment, more perfect than any love I have known since, either for man or woman (WP, p. 257).

Women in Love also brings in explicit physical love between men. It is through the figure of Gerald, however, not Birkin, that we get a sense of the physical presence of man. Poor Birkin is never described physically, being a shadowy, thin, frail creature like Lawrence himself. Gerald, however, is usually seen through Gudrun's eyes. Critics such as Scott Saunders have theorised that Lawrence used Gudrun as his *alter ego*, to describe his own feelings for Gerald. Unlike Connie's feelings for Parkin, they are not really the comments of a woman in love with a man. Gudrun receives no gratification, no blissful sex life, she merely stands back and adores:

And her breast was keen with passion for him, he was so beautiful in his male stillness and mystery. It was a certain pure effluence of maleness, like an aroma from his softly, firmly moulded contours, a certain rich perfection of his presence, that touched her with an ecstasy, a thrill of pure intoxication (WL, p. 199).

The sexual type of love is, however, experienced between Gerald and Birkin. Despite the fact that they really hate each other and feel little other than animosity, the electricity that runs between them is not to be discounted, especially as Lawrence, in a separate essay 'Prologue to Women in Love', went to greater lengths to define those feelings. In the novel, the relationship is described:

> There was a pause of strange enmity between the two men, that was very near to love . . . always their talk brought them into deadly nearness of contact, a strange, perilous intimacy which was either hate or love, or both . . . yet the heart of each burned for the other . . . They had not the faintest belief in deep relationship between men and men, and their disbelief prevented any development of their powerful but suppressed friendliness (WL, p. 37).

In another passage, after they fight together, Lawrence describes in more graphic detail the sheer force of the attraction of these two opposites, in language every bit as strong as that used for Parkin and Connie's connection, and much stronger than is ever brought to play on Birkin's feelings for Ursula:

> . . . they became accustomed to each other, to each other's rhythm, they got a kind of mutual physical understanding . . . They seemed to drive their white flesh deeper and deeper against each other, as if they would break into a oneness . . . [Birkin] seemed to penetrate into Gerald's more solid, more diffuse bulk, to interfuse his body through the body of the other, as if to bring it subtly into subjection . . . It was as if Birkin's . . . fine, sublimated energy entered into the flesh of the fuller man, like some potency, casting a fine net, a prison, through the muscles into the very depths of Gerald's physical being. 'I think also that you are beautiful', said Birkin to Gerald, 'and that is enjoyable too. One should enjoy what one is given.' 'You think I am beautiful – how do you mean, physically? . . . Is this the Bruderschaft you

wanted?' 'Perhaps.' 'Do you think this pledges anything?' 'I don't know', laughed Gerald (WL, pp. 304–8).

Lawrence explores at length the relationship between these two men in the essay 'Prologue to Women in Love', which he wrote for the American edition and then suppressed its publication till after his death. In some ways, what he wrote here was much more shocking than the novel which actually shocked the public. I shall quote it at length, as the evidence included on Lawrence's psyche is very significant. Lawrence's discussion of Birkin has to be his own confessional:

> All the time, he [Birkin] recognised that, although he was always drawn to women, feeling more at home with a woman than with a man, yet it was for men that he felt the hot, flushing, roused attraction which a man is supposed to feel for the other sex . . . the male physique had a fascination for him, and for the female physique he felt only a fondness, a sort of sacred love, as for a sister.
>
> In the street, it was the men who roused him by their flesh and their manly, vigorous movement, quite apart from all the individual character . . . It was the man's physique which held the passion and mystery to him . . . He wanted all the time to love women . . . this was an entanglement from which there seemed no escape . . . He loved his friend, the beauty of whose manly limbs made him tremble with pleasure. He wanted to caress him . . .
>
> In his mind was a small gallery of such men: men whom he had never spoken to, but who had flashed themselves upon his senses unforgettably . . . those white-skinned, keen-limbed men with eyes like blue-flashing ice . . . and then the men with dark eyes that one can enter and plunge into, bathe in, as in a liquid darkness, dark-skinned, supple, night-smelling men, who are the living substance of the viscious universal heavy darkness . . .
>
> There would come into a restaurant a strange Cornish type of man . . . Then again Birkin would feel the desire spring up in him, the desire to know this man, to have him, as it were to eat him, to take the very substance of him . . .
>
> And then in his soul would succeed a sort of despair, because this passion for a man had recurred in him. It was a deep misery to him. And it would seem as if he had always loved men, always

and only loved them . . . 'I should not feel like this', and 'It is the ultimate mark of my own deficiency, that I feel like this . . .' He never accepted the desire and received it as a part of himself. He always tried to keep it expelled from him (P, pp. 103–7).

After that, no further explanation is needed. Lawrence sums up his conflicts and paradoxes better than can any critic.

It was not only Birkin who experienced such adoration for Gerald. Lawrence draws on similar feelings for Kate's desire of Cipriano – in him, it is the dark primitive male – for Connie of Parkin; and for a more blatantly homosexual experience in the short story 'The Prussian Officer'. This story gave Lawrence legal trouble, with its more explicit theme of homosexuality in the army:

> The officer tried hard not to admit the passion that had got hold of him. He would not know that this feeling for his orderly was anything but that of a man incensed by his own stupid, perverse servant. So, keeping quite justified and conventional in his consciousness, he let the other thing run on. His nerves, however, were suffering. At last he slung the end of his belt in his servant's face. When he saw the youth start back, the pain-tears in his eyes and the blood in his mouth, he had felt at once a thrill of deep pleasure and of shame ('The Prussian Officer' and other stories (London: Penguin, 1976), p. 12).

That story is much more conventional in its homosexual theme: the brute male, the tendency to sadism underlying it. Albeit it is a very powerful passage of the emotions. In both *The Plumed Serpent* and *John Thomas and Lady Jane* Lawrence gave to the women his own experience of homoerotic feelings.

Of the many passages that adulate the dark, instinctive primitive men of Quetzalcoatl in *The Plumed Serpent*, one that is not put directly in Kate's voice unfolds the mysteries of that variety of manliness to the reader:

> Their heads were black, their bodies soft and ruddy with the peculiar Indian beauty that has at the same time something terrible in it. The soft, full, handsome torsos of silent men with heads softly bent a little forward; the soft, easy shoulders, that are yet so broad, and which balance upon so powerful a backbone;

shoulders drooping a little, with the relaxation of slumbering, quiescent power; the beautiful ruddy skin, gleaming with a dark fineness; the strong breasts, so male and so deep, yet without the muscular hardening that belongs to white men; . . . all this was strangely impressive, moving strange, frightening emotions in the soul . . . (PS, p. 130).

For Connie, it is the white flesh of Parkin that turns her, or Lawrence, on: 'The white torso of the man had seemed so beautiful to her, opening on the gloom. The white, firm, divine body, with its silky ripple, the white arch of life, as it bent forward over the water, seemed, she could not help it, of the world of gods . . . She had seen beauty, and beauty alive (JTLJ, p. 51).

Lawrence's need for social conformism may have kept him from expressing his homosexual feelings in the reality of his own life, but there was also the conflict within him that his attraction to men was not only physical. He genuinely hoped to improve the world, and the relationship between people, by bringing men closer together in an open and honest type of friendship, a sort of brotherhood. His friendship with John Middleton Murry, the writer and husband of Katherine Mansfield, was the nearest he came in his adult life to reaching his own ideal; though it was always short of the mark. In many of Lawrence's letters he discusses this attitude towards friendship – with Murry himself or with other friends. In May 1917, he wrote to Murry: 'You shouldn't say you love me. You disliked me intensely when you were here, and also at Mylor. But why should we hate or love? We are two separate beings, representing what we represent separately. Yet even if we are opposites, even if at the root we are hostile – I don't say we are – there is no reason why we shouldn't meet somewhere' (L, 23 May 1917). In December 1918, he wrote to Katherine Mansfield, with whom he had an equally electric, hostile relationship:

I do believe in friendship. I believe tremendously in friendship between man and man, a pledging of men to each other inviolably. But I have not ever met or formed such friendship. Also I believe the same way in friendship between men and women, and between women and women, sworn, pledged, eternal, as eternal as the marriage bond, and as deep. But I have not met or formed such friendship (L, December 1918).

In both of those letters, we can hear echoes of Birkin and Gerald – the friendship was more an ideal in Lawrence's head, as was the perfect union with a woman, than a reality.

His hostility towards Middleton Murry is well-documented, coming to a head over Lawrence's desire to set up an ideal community, called Ranamin, in Taos, New Mexico. Middleton Murry, after Katherine Mansfield's death, was supposed to join Lawrence and Frieda, along with Dorothy Brett, but Murry vacillated, havered, and annoyed Lawrence. A letter of February 1924 to Jack:

> Don't think you are doing something for me . . . Move for yourself alone. Decide for yourself in your backbone. I don't really want any allegiance or anything of that sort. I don't want any pact . . . But if you want to go with Frieda and me and Brett *encore bien!* One can but try, and I'm willing . . . Let us clear away all nonsense. I don't *need* you. That is not true, I need nobody. Neither do you need me. If you pretend to need me, you will hate me for it (L, 7 February 1924).

In that same period, when he was having such trouble with people, with all of his friends – the Brett, Murry, and Frieda – he wrote to Dorothy Brett, who was hovering between friendship and wanting to love Lawrence:

> And a word about friendship. Friendship between a man and a woman, as a thing of importance to either, is impossible: and I know it. We are creatures of two halves, spiritual and sensual . . . Your friendship for —— was spiritual, you dragged sex in and he hated you. He'd have hated you anyway. The hatefulness of your friendship I also hate, and between you and me there is no sensual correspondence . . . No, Brett. I do *not* want your friendship, till you have a full relationship somewhere, a kindly relation of both halves (L, January 1925).

Finally, though the letters may not be widely accepted for use in defence of literary criticism, they do provide very valuable support and back-up to the ideas of what Lawrence the man, rather than the writer, was experiencing. He sent off this barb to Murry, shortly before his death.

[May 1929] If I am the only man in your life, it is not because I am I, but merely because I provided the speck of dust on which you formed your crystal of an imaginary man. We don't known one another – if you knew *how* little we know one another! . . . Believe me we belong to different worlds, different ways of consciousness, you and I, and the best we can do is to let one another alone, for ever and ever. We are a dissonance (L, 20 May 1929).

Thus Lawrence failed with his idealised form of male friendship, in his own life. In his novels, he gave the ideas to be voiced by many of his male characters. The strange novel *Kangaroo*, in which Richard Somers and the improbable Kangaroo try to work out a friendship, spells it most clearly. In the novels written in this section of Lawrence's life, beginning with *Women in Love*, but really picking up pace with *Aaron's Rod* and *Kangaroo*, Lawrence is mostly redefining men's relationships with each other.

[Somers] All his life he had cherished a beloved ideal of friendship – David and Jonathan. And now, when true and good friends offered, he found he simply could not commit himself, even to simple friendship . . . He couldn't go along with it. He didn't want a friend, he didn't want loving affection, he didn't want comradeship . . . Yet he wanted *some* living fellowship with other men; as it was he was just isolated. Maybe a living fellowship! – but not affection, not love, not comradeship. Not mates and equality and mingling. Not blood-brotherhood. None of that (K, pp. 119–20).

That jaundiced view can be compared with the more hopeful theorising of Birkin, with Gerald in *Women in Love*. Birkin: 'You've got to take down the love-and-marriage ideal from its pedestal. We want something broader. I believe in the additional perfect relationship between man and man – additional to marriage' (WL, pp. 397–8). Or, as Birkin honestly confesses to Ursula, at the end of the novel: 'You are enough for me, as far as a woman is concerned. You are all women to me. But I wanted a man friend, as eternal as you and I are eternal . . . to make it complete, really happy, I wanted eternal union with a man too: another kind of love', he said (WL, p. 541).

By the time Lawrence came to write *Kangaroo*, he and Frieda had spent longer together on the road, living, loving and quarrelling. His need for male friendship was greater, but also he was more cynical. His attitude to homosexuality was also more frank. He was reading Walt Whitman by now, and finding refreshing idealism in those very homosexual poems:

> Our society is based on the family, the love of a man for his wife and his children, or for his mother and brothers. The family is our social bedrock and limit. Whitman said the next, broader, more unselfish rock should be the Love of Comrades. The sacred relation of a man to his mate, his fellow-man . . . [society] must accept this new relationship as the new sacred social bond, beyond the family (K, p. 219).

In one of the fraught conversations between Somers and Kangaroo, there are strong similarities to the tensions expressed in the letters from Lawrence to Murry: an awareness of failure and a middle-aged desperation:

> [Somers] 'Don't love me. Don't want me to love you. Let's be hard, separate men. Let's understand one another deeper than love'.
> 'Two human ants, in short', said Kangaroo, and his face was yellow.
> 'No, no. Two men. Let us go to the understanding that is deeper than love'.
> 'Is any understanding deeper than love?' asked Kangaroo with a sneer.
> 'Why, yes, you know it is. At least between men . . . you're such a Kangaroo, wanting to carry mankind in your belly-pouch, cosy, with its head and long ears peeping out . . . let's get off it and be men, with the gods beyond us' (K, p. 233).

In *Aaron's Rod*, we see a similar note of desperation at the sadness that the relationship, demanding and involving, between two men, does not seem to work. Lilly has put Aaron to the test. Would the younger man be able to give what his friend demanded? The answer is no. Aaron, scared of involvement, rejects the deep friendship and in turn is thrown out:

> [Lilly] 'I'm *not* going to pretend to have friends on the face of

things. No, and I *don't* have friends who don't fundamentally agree with me. A friend means one who is at one with me in matters of life and death. And if you're at one with all the rest, then you're their friend, not mine. So be *their* friend. And please leave me in the morning' . . . Aaron did not find his friend at home when he called. He felt it was a slap in the face. But then he knew perfectly well that Lilly had made a certain call upon his, Aaron's, soul: a call which he, Aaron, did not intend to obey (AR, pp. 146–7).

What cannot be denied, however, is that behind this adulation of the male, this desire for friendship, for love, for sex, whatsoever, lay a tendency in Lawrence's later life to hate in women what he used to admire, and to fight instead for the supremacy of the male above the female. In encouraging men to fight back and not be dominated by women, to be examined more in the next chapter, Lawrence also seemed to be sliding towards a political viewpoint prevalent in his day; towards a fascist ideal of super-manhood, glorifying the brute, the callous, the violent, as a statement of male power. *The Plumed Serpent*, for example, is a novel in which he celebrates the rebirth of natural man, the return of the repressed male, the rise of the phallus, in its symbolic sense, to take over the world again. Lawrence's travels had witnessed Communist uprisings in Italy and Spain and, despite his early hatred and anger at the war, which had made him desperate to leave England, in 1924 he said that he saw in Germany, a country which had become 'manly again, a bit dangerous, in a manly way . . . the old fierceness coming back'. Lawrence's cult of the male here seemed to come dangerously close to the time of Hitler's actions in Munich, and his fictional heroes in a sense foreshadowed a character such as Hitler. His own view of a saviour was often seen in military terms or in political strong men, such as Robespierre, Danton, Saint-Jerome, Frederick of Asissi, Hannibal, Julius Caesar, Charlemagne and Napoleon.

This has led critics to a theory that Lawrence was compensating for his social and sexual impotence by becoming a priest to the phallic god, a transmitter of supernatural male power, if only through his novels. His fiction is littered with men who are dominated by women, and the reader can easily sense Lawrence's own sexual and social insecurity. Not only did he probably become impotent with his wife, but, by exiling himself from his native land, spending years travelling, creating neither home nor family, he was also socially impotent. Small wonder then that he was, in his last tortured years, driven to associate his sexual insecurity with masculinity and the power ideal. In a letter to Frieda's mother, in 1923, while husband and wife were temporarily separated, he wrote, 'Frieda doesn't understand that a man must be a hero these days, and not only a husband: husband also but more' (SS, p, 140). He began to write in favour of male dominance at home and in the state.

It is in *Aaron's Rod* that he writes most clearly about the hero figure, and the rediscovery of a male culture. Lawrence has turned away here from what he saw as the importance of the 'feminine point of view': that way of life that celebrated the natural, the primitive, mythological, instinctual, sensitive rather than intellectual, feeling rather than rational, mode of being. Now he is writing in favour of 'male' culture, with its symbols, it hardness, its dominance of women. Aaron goes to Florence, and has this experience of the medieval town:

> Aaron felt a new self, a new life-surge rising inside himself. Florence seemed to start a new man in him. It was a town of men . . . all farmers, landowners and land-workers . . . And above all, this sharp, almost acrid, mocking expression, the silent curl of the nose, the eternal challenge, the rock-bottom unbelief, and the subtle fearlessness . . . But men, Men! A town of men, in spite of everything . . . men who existed without apology and without justification . . . Just men (AR, pp. 254–5).

Aaron's attempts at living by this new creed, helped by Rawdon Lilly, fail. At the very end of the novel, Lilly, again in desperation at Aaron's inability to let go into the new life, (compare Aaron's lack of courage with Alvina Houghton's brave striding-out into the unknown in *The Lost Girl*), brings on this scourge:

> [Lilly] 'You, Aaron, you too have the need to submit. You, too, have the need livingly to yield to a more heroic soul, to give yourself. You know you have. And you know it isn't love. It is life-submission. And you know it. But you kick against the pricks. And perhaps you'd rather die than yield. And so, die you must. It is your affair' . . . 'And who shall I submit to?' he said.
> 'Your soul will tell you', replied the other (AR, p. 347).

To many, the ending of this novel is too inconclusive to be a good ending. But Aaron is left in the air because he was unable to be courageous – as indeed was poor Lawrence.

For a psychological interpretation of why Lawrence came to think this way, I turn again to Norman Mailer who, in his *Prisoner of Sex*, was replying to Kate Millett's criticisms of Lawrence. Mailer, like Lawrence, has many ambivalent theories on masculinity and femininity in his own writing. We can feel his sympathy for Lawrence, the man, in these words. He paints a picture of Lawrence, the mother's son, battling with himself, his psyche, his sexuality, and his own confusions:

> For his mind was possessed of that intolerable masculine pressure to command which develops in sons outrageously beloved by their mothers – to be the equal of a woman at twelve or six or any early age which reaches equilibrium between the will of the son and the will of the mother, strong love to strong love, is all but to guarantee the making of a tyrant . . . Hitlers develop out of such imbalance derived from imbalance . . .
>
> . . . he had become a man by an act of will, he was bone and blood of the classic family stuff out of which homosexuals are made, he had lifted himself out of his natural destiny which was probably to have the sexual life of a woman, had diverted the virility of his brain down into some indispensible minimum of phallic force – no wonder he worshipped the phallus, he above all men knew what an achievement was its rise from the root, its assertion to stand proud on a delicate base . . .
>
> . . . he flirts with homosexuality, but is secretly, we may assume, obsessed with it. For he is still in need of that restorative sex he can no longer find, and since his psyche was originally shaped to be homosexual, homosexuality could yet be his peace . . . Homosexuality becomes a double irony – he must now seek to dominate men physically more powerful than himself . . .
>
> But homosexuality would have been the abdication of Lawrence as a philosopher-king. Conceive how he must have struggled against it! . . . He has been a victim of love, and will die for lack of the full depth of a woman's love for him – what a near to infinite love he had needed (NM, pp. 153–9).

8 Hatred of Women

Lawrence's life was dominated by thought of the relationship between men and women, and the knowledge that gender roles were going to have to be redefined in the modern world. To a pioneer of this type of thinking, some of the confusions in his own heart must have been obstacles. Rational acceptance of a new mode of thinking is often far removed even from one's own subconscious acceptance of the ideas. Thus while Lawrence theorised about the feminine point of view, and the importance of men awakening to the feminine instinct, at the same time he was fighting the idea with the acceptance of previous generations that men were really the most powerful sex. Add to that the problems that Lawrence, the man, experienced in his own life: his battle with an ambivalent sexuality that at times appeared as repressed homosexuality; his struggle to find deep friendship with a man, which to him would not be physical; and, at the same time, his effort to keep up a deeper commitment to woman. By early middle age he was exhausted. He had the battle, too, with the continual ill health which would have sapped confidence in his maleness from the biggest and strongest male of the species, and left Lawrence always small, weak and unquestionably emotionally impotent.

In his heart, Lawrence still felt that a man should be involved in manly pursuits. Yet he had taken the opposite path, as a writer, an artist, a thinker. He travelled, never set up home or family, and could not even control his own wife. Whether he became physically impotent as well, is a matter of speculation. We can take as evidence what he wrote about Frieda, and their sexual relationship, in a letter to Katherine Mansfield in December 1918. The letter was written after the Lawrences had been together ten years, and twelve years before his death – suggesting he had had many years of disillusionment with the man–woman relationship in his middle age. The letter refers to this theme of man against woman, whom he began to see as the Magna Mater, or devouring mother:

In a way, Frieda is the devouring mother. It is awfully hard, once the sex relation has gone this way, to recover. If we don't recover, we die. But Frieda says I'm antediluvian in my positive attitude. I do think a woman must yield some sort of precedence to a man, and he must take his precedence. I do think men must go ahead absolutely in front of their women . . . Consequently, the women must follow as it were unquestioningly. I can't help it, I do believe this, Frieda doesn't. Hence our fight (MG, p. 133).

The exigencies of his debilitating illness in later life and the continued strife with Frieda, despite their never-ending commitment to each other, cannot have made sex easy for either of them. My speculation on the facts of his real life goes no further, for the spiritual impotence he suffered was more than enough to encourage his ideas, towards the end of his life, to shift a few degrees. Once the balance of that equality, so much explored, was broken, then women appeared to him to have taken over. To some degree, towards the end of his life, he fought back; trying desperately to return to men some of the supremacy which he felt had existed in more primitive societies.

As a theme, the dominated man appears throughout Lawrence's novels. Scott Saunders, in *The World of the Major Novels*, lists the men ruled by women, in both the earliest and the latest novels: old man Morel, Paul, Will Brangwen, Skrebensky, Gerald, Aaron, Rawdon, Ricio (in 'St Mawr'), Basil ('The Ladybird') and Clifford Chatterley. Sometimes Lawrence attacks the emasculating woman and arranges for her her just deserts. Usually, the emasculating woman shows up what is lacking in the men who allow themselves to be dominated.

In the early novels, it is his male characters who have fallen prey to industrialisation who come in for criticism. They have lost their passion and will. They have become content to be mastered by their bosses in the new technological age, living only for ideas and money. Leslie, whom Lettie marries in *The White Peacock*, is described as just another dull industrialist, which immediately explains why he is no match for Lettie. But even George is weakened by Lettie, so that he loses out in the battle between the sexes: 'his strength had gone . . . he walked weakly', and he turned to drink for solace. In *The Rainbow*, there are many dominated men, but Will Brangwen stands out most obviously as the one led into love and passion by Anna; 'He let her do as she liked with him . . .

He was translated with gladness to be in her hands'. Then, when Anna continues to rule by producing babies, Will is subservient to her and the child, 'he served the little matriarchy, nursing the child and helping with the housework, indifferent any more of his own dignity and importance. . . . He was not what is called a manly man: he did not drink or smoke or arrogate importance' (R, p. 208).

Winifred Inger, the lesbian, with whom the young Ursula had a teenage homosexual experience, is given an interesting comment on modern men, and how they have lost their 'spunk'. Maybe she is given the words to explain why she became homosexual. Whatever the reason, whether Lawrence approves of her as a woman or not, she is allowed to put men down very severely: 'The men will do no more, – they have lost the capacity for doing . . . They make everything fit into an old, inert idea. . . . They don't come to one and love one, they come to an idea, and they say "You are my idea" . . . they are all impotent, they can't *take* a woman' (R, p. 343). It is industry that has sapped them, 'the pit owns every man. The women have what is left. . . . The pit takes all that really matters'(R, p. 349).

At this stage in his writing, Lawrence was still very concerned with maleness and its dry, unimaginative state as compared to femaleness. Gudrun on Gerald: 'His maleness bores me. Nothing is so boring, so inherently stupid and stupidly conceited . . . '. 'I don't worship Loerke, but at any rate, he is a free individual. He is not stiff with conceit of his own maleness' (WL, p. 521). Birkin, listening to her, reflects on the time he stared at the dead stallion, when he had seen it as a dead mass of maleness, 'repugnant'. Lou Witt, in the story 'St Mawr', which introduced Lawrence's later themes of finding salvation for modern ills in primitive societies, finds what she wants of maleness in the horse called St Mawr. It is in the horse that she senses the wild, free, independent spirit that she has always associated with manliness, but which she had never found in men. Lou takes the horse to foreign lands, to the wild western states of America, and discovers the primitive power she has been looking for; just as Lawrence had found it in New Mexico among the native Indians. Lou says to her mother, the equally indomitable Mrs Witt:

> I don't admire the cave man, and that sort of thing. But think, mother, if we could get our lives straight from the source, as the animals do, and still be ourselves. You don't like men yourself.

But you've no idea how men just tire me out: even the very thought of them. You say they are too animal. But they're not, mother. It's the animal in them has gone perverse, or cringing, or humble, or domesticated like dogs. I don't know one single man who is a proud living animal (SM (Octopus edn), p. 333).

The image of modern man being like the domesticated dog is used several times. Lou says with considerable wit, about the fear of losing her husband, 'I should say: "Miss Manby, you may have my husband, but not my horse. My husband won't need emasculating and my horse I won't have you meddle with. I'll preserve one last male thing in the museum of this world, if I can" ' (SM, p. 359). Yvette, the girl in 'The Virgin and the Gipsy', is also looking for maleness and she finds it in the wild primitive spirit of the gipsies. It makes Yvette feel embarrassed at her own weakness in going with these modern young men: 'she would have the same contempt for Daddy and for Uncle Fred, as men, as she would have for fat old slobbery Rover, the Newfoundland dog. A great, sardonic female contempt, for such domesticated dogs, calling themselves men' (VG, p. 723). Later, at a dance, Yvette, supposedly finding her true mate among the local boys, feels anger and pride:

How dared he look at her like that? So she gazed glaringly at the insipid beaux on the dancing-floor. And she despised him. Just as the raggle-taggle gipsy women despise men who are not gipsies, despise their dog-like walk down the streets, she found herself despising this crowd. Where among them was the subtle, lonely, insinuating challenge that could reach her? She did not want to mate with a house-dog (VG, p. 732).

Much of Lawrence's writing is given, however, to actual explicit invective against women: direct hatred and anger, roused by fear of their emasculating power. Such comments have been picked up by some female critics as the mainstream of his writing. Kate Millett, for instance, obviously saw Lawrence as a man who hated women, and whose literary output was devoted to castigating women. Simone de Beauvoir criticises Lawrence, saying that his only concern was to show women how to be mastered (SB, pp. 249–54). But his themes and his involvement in the subject are much more complex than that. To take one passage from *Aaron's Rod*, in which Aaron describes the relationship he had with Lottie that made him walk out from home, we can see how the other side to Lawrence's optimism about duality, and the ever-present battle in the relationship between men and women – the negative to the positive – could predominate and become tiring, enervating or downright destructive to men.

In Aaron, the sense of defeat gives him the will to survive, to go all out for the protection of his maleness. This is the theme behind much of Lawrence's later writing:

> Come life, come death, she too would never yield . . . He too would never yield. The illusion of love was gone forever. Love was a battle in which each party strove for the mastery of the other's soul. So far, man had yielded the mastery to woman. Now he was fighting for it back again . . . But whether the woman yielded or not, he would keep the mastery of his own soul and conscience and actions . . . Henceforth, life single, not life double. He looked at the sky, and thanked the universe for the blessedness of being alone in the universe. To be alone, to be oneself, not to be driven or violated into something which is not oneself, surely it is better than anything . . . Let there be clean and pure division first, perfected singleness. That is the only way to final, living unison: through sheer, finished singleness (AR, pp. 155–6).

Many years later, Lawrence wrote an essay on the Matriarchy, published only shortly before his death in 1928, under the title 'If Women Were Supreme'. The influence, noted earlier, of Bachofen's *Das Mutterecht* can be assumed in the intellectual content but, for the emotional content, we have to look no further than the later novels. Lawrence wrote:

> [Modern man] is afraid of being swamped, turned into a mere accessory of bare-limbed, swooping woman; swamped by numbers, swamped by her devouring energy. He talks rather bitterly about rule of women, monstrous regiment of women, and about matriarchy, and, rather feebly, about man being master again . . . Woman has emerged, and you can't put her back again . . . It is said that in the ancient dawn of history there was nothing but matriarchy: children took the mother's name, belonged to the mother's clan, and the man was nameless . . . To satisfy his deeper social instincts and intuitions, a man must be able to get

away from his family, and from women altogether . . . let man get free again, free from the tight littleness of family and family possessions. Give woman her full independence, and with it, the full responsibility of her independence (P, pp. 549–53).

It is an interesting quote that casts light on Lawrence's own support of female emancipation. Only through the independence of women can men also find their emancipation – freedom from family, from too much responsibility, from too much control by first mother, then wife.

It is in *Aaron's Rod* that we find most of Lawrence's thought and feeling on the subject of ruined manhood. The novel is not very widely read, but it is valuable for what it reveals of this stage in Lawrence's development. Aaron, one of Lawrence's few male characters who is allowed to explore and develop his own sense of identity, wanders through life, after leaving wife and family, meeting another man whom he sees as his leader; trying to find what his true feelings are. At the beginning, Aaron is full of hatred for women:

'Why, you know – . . . they look on a man as if he was nothing but an instrument to get and rear children. If you have anything to do with a woman, she thinks it's because you want to get children by her. And I'm damned if it is. I want my own pleasure, or nothing; and children be damned . . . They make a criminal of you. Them and their children be cursed. Is my life given me for nothing but to get children, and work for a woman? . . . Be damned and blasted to women and all their importances', cried Aaron. 'They want to get you under, and children is their weapon'.

'Men have got to stand up to the fact that manhood is more than childhood – and then force women to admit it', said Lilly . . . 'The man's spirit has gone out of the world. Men can't move an inch unless they can grovel humbly at the end of the journey' (AR, pp. 123–4).

The dialogue between Aaron and Rawdon Lilly centres on what women have done to men, and what is men's course of exploration. Lilly is hostile and cynical, where Aaron tends to be dejected and depressed, by the weight of his oppression from women. Lilly at one point recounts a story from Josephine Ford, a liberated modern young woman, whom both know. Josephine had confessed to Lilly there was no such thing as love, she only wanted men because of her fear of being alone. 'A woman is like a violinist: any fiddle, any instrument rather than empty hands and no tune going' (AR, p. 131). To Aaron himself, all his wife's grumbles and accusations of unhappiness he has caused her to suffer, come from her deep-rooted belief in female power: ' . . . under all her whimsicalness and fretfulness was a conviction as firm as steel; that she, as woman, was the centre of creation, the man was but an adjunct. She, as woman, and particularly as mother, was the first great source of life and being, and also of culture. The man was but the instrument and the finisher. She was the source and the substance' (AR, p. 192). Aaron is a fighter, and Lawrence gives him hope; to go on beyond this stalemate: 'But in Aaron was planted another seed. He did not know it . . . Born in him was a spirit which could not worship woman: no, and would not. Could not and would not. It was not in him . . . through his plaintive and homage rendering love of a young husband was always, for the woman, discernible the arrogance of self-unyielding male. He never yielded himself: never . . . And he outraged her!' (AR, p. 193).

One of Lawrence's most vindictive statements against women comes in *The Plumed Serpent*. He is writing about Kate Leslie as the middle-aged modern woman who has the chance to find what Lou Witt in 'St Mawr' sought – salvation through primitive man in touch with his instinctive maleness. So Kate tries to work out whether she could really renounce her past life for this fearful one, implying complete submission to the powerful male force, and she reflects on the women she has known and left behind:

> Another thing, she had observed, with a touch of horror. One after the other, her women 'friends', the powerful love-women, at the age of forty, forty-five, fifty, they lost all their charm and allure, and turned into real grimalkins, greyish, avid, and horrifying, prowling around looking for prey that became scarcer and scarcer. . . . It is all very well for a woman to cultivate her ego, her individuality. It is all very well for her to despise love, or to love love as a cat loves a mouse . . . to vivify her own individuality and voluptuously fill the belly of her own ego.
>
> 'Woman has suffered far more from the suppression of her ego than from sex suppression' says a woman writer, and it may well be true. But look, only look at the modern woman of fifty and

fifty-five, those who have cultivated their ego to the top of their bent! Usually, they are grimalkins to fill one with pity or with repulsion (PS, p. 456).

The last word, however, should be given to Mellors, in *Lady Chatterley's Lover*, who has been so wounded by his relationships with women, that when he and Connie are first drawn together the last thing he wants is to become involved with another woman. Like Aaron, he has opted for singleness, having decided that that is the only way for his ego, and his sense of individuality, to stay alive. By the time of *Lady Chatterley's Lover*, Lawrence has determined to write again about sex, whether because of his own sexual problems or not we can only surmise. Mellors is smarting strongly from the blows to his male sexual pride from his former wife Bertha Coutts. It is a familiar theme by now: the hatred of a woman who takes too much control, who tries to dominate the man:

> That was what I wanted: a woman who *wanted* me to fuck her. So I fucked her like a good un. . . . But she treated me with insolence. And she got so's she'd never have me when I wanted her: never. Always put me off, brutal as you like. . . . But when I had her, she'd never come-off when I did. Never! She'd just wait. . . . And when I'd come and really finished, then she'd start on her own account, and I had to stop inside her till she brought herself off, wriggling and shouting, she'd clutch clutch with herself down there, an' then she'd come off, fair in ecstasy. And then she'd say: That was lovely! . . . She sort of got harder and harder to bring off, and she's sort of tear at me down there, as if it was a beak tearing at me. By God, you think a woman's soft down there, like a fig. . . . Self! Self! Self! all self! tearing and shouting! . . . That's how old whores used to be, so men used to say (LCL, pp. 210-11).

Mellor's train of thought expands into assuming that all such modern women are really lesbian, and remembering many of these lesbian types he has come across. With Connie, he has found a woman who wants to explore a relationship with *him*, which means she is prepared to lose some of her ego and individuality to him; and vice versa. With Connie, however, he also comes across a different problem. Because she is of superior class, and has more money, again its seems that he is going to be dominated by her, albeit in a different way. He gets anxious and worried about the implications of their trying to come together in life. She wants their sex life desperately and he fears her active participation. He shouts at her, 'I can't just be your male concubine . . . The money is yours, the position is yours, the decisions will lie with you. I'm not just my Lady's fucker, after all' (LCL, p. 289).

One of Lawrence's ultimate statements about his fear of women, his hatred of them, and the vengeance he seeks over them, comes in the story 'The Woman Who Rode Away'. This woman, and her kind of womanhood, are brutally sacrificed by the primitive male: obliterated by the great primeval symbols towering over the 'fallen individual independence of woman'. It is Pan worship, nature love. The self-willed, dominating woman, is there lying prone beneath the pyre, naked 'in a state of barbaric ecstasy' ('The Woman Who Rode Away', p. 69). One can almost feel the force of this fantasy as it played in Lawrence's mind.

So to the final stage, in which Lawrence turns full circle and advocates the theory of male supremacy: the ultimate fight back. In his early writings, this theme is linked to the instances of homosexual reverence and adoration of the male, but by the later writings it has emerged as a strong call to men to find themselves and take over again. It is a theme that has to be understood, alongside all his writing about women.

One of the earliest instances of this passion for sheer maleness, comes in contradictory fashion in his evocation of Gerald in *Women in Love*. Sometimes Lawrence seems to be criticising Gerald, and other times adoring him. Gerald, in the famous scene with the horse that is trying to bolt, is shown as a true exponent of clear, precise, cruel, male dominance: 'Gudrun was as if numbed in her mind by the sense of indomitable soft weight of the man, bearing down into the living body of the horse . . . into pure control; a sort of soft white magnetic domination from the loins and thighs and calves, . . . into unutterable subordination' (WL, p. 126).

By the time of writing *Aaron's Rod* and *Kangaroo*, Lawrence has emerged as the defender of malehood against women. Here he cites his new theory that women must submit to the new man if they are to find salvation. *Aaron's Rod*, at the end, has these prophetic words:

Whatever else happens, somewhere, sometime, the deep power-urge in man will have to issue forth again, and woman will submit livingly, not subjectedly . . . Woman – and man too. Yield to the deep power-soul in the individual man, and obey implicitly . . . I do believe that every man must fulfill his own soul, every woman must be herself, herself only, not some man's instrument, or some embodied theory (AR, pp. 346-7).

In *Kangaroo*, Somers tries to explain to his wife that he is reaching out from the confines of their marriage to find something in the male world: 'You see', he said, 'I have the roots of my life with you. But I want if possible to send out a new shoot in the life of mankind – the effort man makes forever, to grow into new forms' (K. p. 78).

Kate, in *The Plumed Serpent*, feels this new male force very keenly: 'Kate felt she was in the presence of men. Here were men face to face, not with death and self-sacrifice, but with the life-issue. She felt, for the first time in her life, a pang almost like fear, of men who were passing beyond what she knew, beyond her depth' (PS, p. 73). She finds it in Cipriano. He sums up the dark passionate male, who is going to take over the world – after all, the blonde men were dying, 'their bravery and supremacy was leaving, going into the hands of the dark men, who were rousing at last'.

Cipriano is an exponent of phallic power – this is Lawrence's ultimate weapon in the artillery of male victory. In men, in the phallus, lies the key to the instinctive world, the key to the force that will bring passion and energy and the life force back into the world. You can criticise Lawrence for placing the emphasis on the phallus, rather than on the female genitals, but remember that this argument is *against* the matriarchal womb worship which he has previously espoused and in which he found himself drowning. Now, as an escape, he looks to the phallus as the root – the beginning of male salvation.

The mystery of the primeval world! . . . Cipriano was still a power. Once you entered his mystery the scale of all things changed, and he became a living male power, undefined, and unconfined . . . As he sat in silence, casting the old, twilit, Pan-power over her, she felt herself submitting, succumbing. . . . It was the ancient mystery, the ancient god-devil of the male Pan. . . . Ah! and what a mystery of prone submission, on her part, this huge erection would imply! Submission absolute . . . (PS, pp. 324–5).

In the Lady Chatterley novels, the mystery of the phallic theory is also explained. Parkin, in *John Thomas and Lady Jane*, explains the mystery to Connie. To him the phallus is a godhead, and again the saviour of both men and women. But in the Lady Chatterley novels, Lawrence has worked this theory of male supremacy in with his former leaning towards the importance of the feminine point of view, towards the coming together of both sexes, in submission to each other. What is interesting about Parkin and Connie is that together they explore a new kind of maleness – this is finally Lawrence's answer. Maleness is to be redefined, is to discover its instinctive primitive power, and the way to that is for modern man to admit to the femaleness within him. Parkin worships the phallus, but he also knows how mistakenly other men have interpreted its power:

> And this godhead in him had always been wounded, yet even now was not dead. In most men it was dead. To most men, the penis was merely a member, at the disposal of the personality. Most men merely used their penis as they use their fingers, for some personal purpose of their own. But in a true man, the penis has a life of its own, and is the second man within the man: the penis is a mere member of the physiological body. But the phallus, in the old sense, has roots, the deepest roots of all, in the soul and the greater consciousness of man, and it is through the phallic roots that inspiration enters the soul (JTLJ, p. 238).

Connie even tells her sister Hilda how much she has learned by giving way to the phallic supremacy: inspiration and wisdom come from the root.

> I *know* it is the penis which connects us with the stars and the sea and everything. It is the penis which touches the planets, and makes us feel their special light. I know it. I *know* it was the penis which really put the evening stars into my inside self. I used to *look* at the evening stars, and think how lovely and wonderful it was. But now it's in me as well as outside me, and I hardly need look at it. I *am* it. I don't care what you say, it was the penis gave it me (JTLJ, p. 312).

But maybe the last words should go to Connie, talking to Parkin about his manliness, which is altered by his opening himself up to the female within him, being transformed by femininity and an understanding of the phallic roots of primitive consciousness. There is no danger that Parkin is one of the old-style men, with a hard will and an insistence on knowledge above instinct. Yet Parkin is a wonderful male, and a supreme one, with all the male beauty, sympathy and lovingness, that Lawrence wanted to see in a man and would have liked to have found in a friend for himself:

> [Connie] You say you have too much of a woman in you, you only mean you are more sensitive than stupid people like Dan Coutts. You ought to be proud that you are sensitive, and have that much of a woman's good qualities. It's very good for a man to have a touch of woman's sensitiveness. I hate your stupid hard-headed clowns who think they are so very *manly* (JTLJ, p. 333).

Select Bibliography

Lawrence's works cited in order of publication. The references cited in the text all refer to the paperback editions.

NOVELS

The White Peacock, first published 1911 (London: Penguin, 1974)

Sons and Lovers, first published 1913 (London: Penguin, 1967)

The Rainbow, first published 1915 (London: Penguin, 1975)

The Lost Girl, first published 1920 (London: Penguin, 1976)

Women in Love, first published 1921 (London: Penguin, 1968)

Aaron's Rod, first published 1922 (London: Penguin, 1975)

Kangaroo, first published 1923 (London: Penguin, 1974)

The Plumed Serpent, first published 1926 (London: Penguin, 1974)

Lady Chatterley's Lover, first published 1928 (1960) (London: Pengiun, 1967)

John Thomas and Lady Jane, first published 1954 (London: Pengiun, 1974)

The Boy in The Bush (with M. L. Skinner) (New York: Viking Compass, 1972)

SHORT STORIES

'The Prussian Officer', and other stories, first published 1914 (London: Penguin, 1976)

'Love Among the Haystacks' (London: Penguin, 1975)

'The Woman Who Rode Away', and other stories (London: Penguin, 1975)

'St Mawr', first published 1925 (New York: Heinemann Octopus, 1976)

'The Virgin and the Gipsy', first published 1930 (New York: Heinemann Octopus, 1976)

ESSAYS, LETTERS AND CRITICISM

'Fantasia of the Unconscious' and 'Psychoanalysis and the Unconscious' first published 1923 (London: Penguin, 1975)

Selected Essays (London: Penguin, 1950)

Study of Thomas Hardy, edited by J. H. Davies, first published 1936 (London: Heinemann Educational, 1973)

Phoenix II, edited by Warren Roberts and Harry T. Moore (London: Heinemann, 1968)

The Letters of D. H. Lawrence, edited by Aldous Huxley (London: Heinemann, 1932)

SECONDARY SOURCES

Biography and Autobiography

Ivor Brown, *Shaw in His Time* (London: Nelson, 1965)

Jessie Chambers, *D. H. Lawrence: A Personal Record* (London: Cassell, 1965)

Martin Green, *The von Richtofen Sisters: The Triumphant and the Tragic Modes of Love* (New York: Basic Books, 1974)

Emily Hahn, *Lorenzo: D. H. Lawrence and the women who loved him* (New York: Lippincott, 1975)

Frieda Lawrence, *Not I but the Wind . . .* (London: Chivers, 1964)

Robert Lucas, *Frieda Lawrence, a biography* (London: Secker & Warburg, 1973)

Harry T. Moore, *The Priest of Love: a life of D. H. Lawrence*, first published 1954 (London: Penguin, 1976)

John Middleton Murry, *Son of Woman: The Story of D. H. Lawrence* (London: Cape, 1931)

Frank Swinnerton, *The Georgian Literary Scene 1910–35* (London: Hutchinson, 1969)

CRITICISM

The stable of Lawrence criticism has, of course, been referred to in the study for this book, but not all are listed here. This bibliography contains a list only of those works that have special relevance to the theme of this book, and which are referred to in the text.

Simone de Beauvoir, *The Second Sex* (London: Penguin, 1972)

H. M. Daleski, *The Forked Flame: A Study of D. H. Lawrence* (London: Faber, 1965)

122   *D. H. Lawrence and Women*

Emile Delavenay, *Edward Carpenter and D. H. Lawrence: A Study in Edwardian Transition* (London: Heinemann, 1971)

Carolyn Heilbrun, *Towards Androgyny: Aspects of Male and Female in Literature* (London: Gollancz, 1973)

Norman Mailer, *The Prisoner of Sex* (London: Sphere, 1972)

Kate Millett, *Sexual Politics*, chapter on D. H. Lawrence (London: Abacus, 1972), pp. 237–93

Shiela Rowbotham and Jeffrey Weeks, *Socialism and the New Life: The Personal and Sexual Politics of Edward Carpenter and Havelock Ellis* (London: Pluto Press, 1977)

Scott Saunders, *D. H. Lawrence: The World of the Major Novels* (London: Vision Press, 1973)

Index